MAKE 'EM BELIEVE

The Inside Story of the Badgers' Road to the 2015 Final Four

KCI Sports Publishing   3340 Whiting Avenue, Suite 5
Stevens Point, WI 54481
Phone: 1-800-697-3756   Fax: 715-344-2668

Nicky Brillowski, Book and Cover Design

ISBN: 978-1-940056-25-8

Printed in the United States of America

By David Stluka

FOREWORD *by Frank Kaminsky*

When I sat down to think about my decision to return for my senior season at Wisconsin, a million things started running through my head. I thought about how long I had dreamed about playing in the NBA, how long of a road it had already been to get where I was, and how long the journey would be to get there.

But when I really thought about it, there was one overarching theme: Wisconsin was my home. I was born and raised in the western suburbs of Chicago, a small town called Lisle; but Madison, Wisconsin taught me more about myself than any other place, and if my father taught me anything it is that you don't turn your back on someone or something that has been loyal to you.

What made Wisconsin such a special place for me was not what I achieved on the basketball court. It was how I arrived on campus as an 18-year-old immature boy and then grew into a 22-year-old (slightly more) mature man. Our team not only made it to the highest level in college basketball, but we grew up together and had a blast doing it.

These past two seasons were magical. Not a single person took it for granted, and every person enjoyed it to the maximum. All of the friendships made, all of the memories we forged, and all of the accomplishments we achieved will never be taken away from us – and will never be forgotten.

As I look back on it, it's hard to pick a "greatest basketball memory," because we were lucky enough to have so many. But walking around the court holding up our "Make 'Em Believe" shirt after knocking off Kentucky in the Final Four might be number one on the list.

Seeing the pure elation on everyone's faces solidified the fact that we had etched our names in the annals of college basketball history. Take a minute to think of the story. We lose to Kentucky the previous season in the Final Four on a buzzer beater. We fight hard to return to the biggest stage and take down "one of the greatest teams in college basketball history." Experience vs. Youth. Three-star recruits vs. McDonald's All-Americans. I have a hunch that Wisconsin beating undefeated Kentucky will stick around for quite some time.

Off the court, I can't give you a single greatest memory. I mean that sincerely.

Every single day was a privilege. Our team was a collection of guys who were not afraid to show the world who we really were. We liked having fun, we weren't serious 100 percent of the time, we joked around, we laughed, and we were good at basketball. We didn't see ourselves as teammates. We see ourselves as family. I am proud to say that my family achieved something great.

Now that my time as a student-athlete at the University of Wisconsin-Madison has come to an end, I get a chance to reflect on what being a Badger means to me. Being a Badger isn't just something you say when someone asks you where you went to school. Being a Badger is a way of life that you are proud to live by.

We all went and cheered at football games. We all went and sat at the Terrace and had a Spotted Cow or six. We all dreaded walking up Bascom Hill. We were all part of the magic of the University of Wisconsin, and it is our duty to carry it with us wherever we go. I had the time of my life in Madison. I am not sure if I will ever find the kind of magic that I found at Wisconsin, but I will continue to search for it wherever life takes me.

On, Wisconsin. Forever. ∎

By David Stluka

CONTENTS

Foreword - Frank Kaminsky 4

Prologue 6

The Run That Almost Wasn't 10

I *Can* Believe I'm Going to Say It 14

Butch Ryan 18

Kentucky Blues 20

Great Expectations 24

The Battle 4 Atlantis 28

A Break in Momentum 36

From Bad to Worse 40

Changing of the Guard 42

Untouchable 46

A Forgettable Trip 54

Big Ten Champs 60

Frank The Tank 64

Ohio State-ment 74

Big Ten Champs, Again 78

Captain America 88

The Dance Begins 92

Soundtrack: Laughter 98

Sweet 16: North Carolina 106

Badgers Go Hollywood 110

Arizona: The Sequel 114

The Local Legend 120

The Promised Land Isn't Promised... It's Earned 124

The Architect 136

So Close, So Proud 140

America's Team 150

Epilogue 154

Season Stats 157

Schedule & Results 158

About the Author 159

"Make 'Em Believe"

As the scoreboard at Lucas Oil Stadium in Indianapolis ticked toward 0:00, Frank Kaminsky pointed to his chest and mouthed the words "Make... 'Em... Believe. This is what Make 'Em Believe was about."

Serenaded by the iconic voice of CBS announcer Jim Nantz bellowing, "On Wisconsin... to the National Championship," the Badgers were about to pull off a feat that few outside the Wisconsin locker room thought possible.

While his teammates embraced and jumped near midcourt, Kaminsky thrust his fists toward the cavernous rafters, parading around the Final Four court holding a shirt emblazoned with the words:

"Make 'Em Believe"

A rallying cry that, while rooted in the endearing goofiness of the team, underscored the team's singular focus of reaching college basketball's biggest stage.

That indelible image of Kaminsky, the unlikely consensus national player of the year, standing tall after the Badgers had just knocked off the unbeaten, 38-0, once-in-a-generation Kentucky Wildcats, captured perhaps the greatest moment in Wisconsin basketball history.

Exactly 364 days after suffering a crushing loss to the Wildcats in the 2014 Final Four, Wisconsin's entire motivation was built on returning to this moment and atoning for missed opportunities.

Wisconsin 71, Kentucky 64 was no David vs. Goliath.

Wisconsin 71, Kentucky 64 was no upset.

Wisconsin 71, Kentucky 64 was no fluke.

It was fate.

◆◆◆◆

For Frank Kaminsky and the Badgers, "Make 'Em Believe" was more than a t-shirt slogan.
By Michael Conroy

Even when adidas asked them to wear a different shirt for the postseason, the Badgers stuck with their own message. *By Patrick Herb*

On July 13, 2014, nearly the entire Wisconsin team gathered at a gym in Lisle, Illinois, a 3-point shot from the childhood home of preseason All-American Frank Kaminsky, to work as counselors for a local youth basketball camp. Throughout the day the Badgers players would engage in competition with the campers, aged third through 12th grade.

During a spirited game of knockout, the final two left standing were Kaminsky, the hometown headliner, and relatively unknown soon-to-be-sophomore Vitto Brown. Realizing the odds – and crowd of children – were stacked against Brown, his classmate Bronson Koenig yelled out, "They don't think you can beat him. Make 'em believe V."

Later, when the young campers asked to challenge the reigning 2014 Final Four Badgers, Kaminsky and his teammates were unsure how to approach the game. Instead of letting the kids win, the college boys followed the lead of Brown, "No prisoners. Doesn't matter how young or small they are, treat them like the enemy."

The Badgers played all out, installing a full-court press, rarely letting their miniature counterparts even cross half court. They would steal the ball and immediately lob it to the 7-foot Kaminsky standing under the basket, who would turn and dunk so hard it would send the 10-years olds tumbling over like bowling pins, giggling all the way to the floor.

"They were laughing like it was the greatest time of their lives," Kaminsky remembered. "We liked to think it was our way of giving back to the community."

As best they could, the Wisconsin players tried to keep a straight face despite the one-sided beatdown.

"They think they can play with us, make 'em believe!" Brown blared with a straight face despite cracking up inside.

There it was again, "Make 'Em Believe."

A motto with a backstory as silly as the collection of characters who dreamed it up, those three simple words would follow Wisconsin all season. The last thing the team saw before taking the court at the Kohl Center? "Make 'Em Believe" posted on the locker room wall. The team was asked to wear warm-up shirts for the 2015 postseason, branded with adidas' latest marketing campaign. The team declined, emphatically. They'd stick to their own message. You guessed it… Make 'Em Believe.

Surely the inspiration that took Wisconsin to a program-record 36 wins, an undisputed

Big Ten championship and the 2015 national championship game had to mean something more than convincing their legitimacy to a gym full of preteens, right?

Then came the Badgers' April 5th team huddle. Moments before tipping off against Kentucky in the 2015 Final Four, 15 hands pulled together in unison with the memory of last year's soul-crushing loss still burning in their membranes. Standing at center court of Lucas Oil Stadium, standing in the eye of the Big Blue hurricane that had laid waste to everything in its path, Kaminsky left his teammates with a few final words.

"When you look across that court, do you honestly believe that they have worked as hard as you?" the team captain barked. "Do you really think they have put in the sweat that you have? Do you think they respect you? Do they think we're good enough to beat them? I believe this is our destiny. I believe that we make our own destiny. Let's go out there and make them believe."

Indeed, Make 'Em Believe did mean more. So much more.

"You want to know what Make 'Em Believe is about?" 2015 sophomore Nigel Hayes asked, answering without waiting for a response. "The day we got our 2014 Final Four rings, a pretty high-profile host of an ESPN show actually tweeted out something like, 'I forgot Wisconsin was even in the Final Four.'

"For him to say that is the lack of respect that Make 'Em Believe refers to. There were perceptions about our team that maybe we were lucky to get there the previous year, or that we couldn't do it again or that this program isn't one of the elites. Make 'Em Believe was meant for people who may not have wanted to give us our kudos, but after seeing us beat teams, they literally had no choice but to tip their hat and believe that we're the real deal."

"Make 'Em Believe was about getting people on board with what our beliefs were," Kaminsky went on. "It wasn't so much that we needed to convince people that we're a good team, but more about leaving our mark on our opponents, media, fans, everyone. Forcing them to recognize us."

"You need to make each other believe first," senior and 2015 co-captain Josh Gasser explained. "I think nationally, everyone *thought* we could get back to the Final Four or maybe win a championship. But outside of the team, I don't know if anyone truly *believed* it. We truly *believed* that we could do it and that's all that matters, just the 16 guys in that locker room. We set our goals and no one else has an influence on them. It was just about us."

The 2015 Wisconsin Badgers made believers out of everyone.

On their way to cutting down nets after three different championships, America learned what the entire state of Wisconsin already knew. A team full of under-recruited, over-achievers, the Badgers were everything that's right in sports. Star power and brilliant athletic ability crossed with a juvenile playfulness and joy. The Badgers laughed and appreciated the moments they were living, and we appreciated them right back.

Two days after calling Wisconsin's 68-63 loss to Duke in the national championship, Nantz appeared on the nationally syndicated Dan Patrick Show to reflect on the title bout. After a series of questions about Duke, Nantz asked if he could volunteer one additional thought before transitioning to another topic.

"You can't help but meet, greet and in the end admire some people that you come across. That Wisconsin team – and I've done the NCAA tournament for 30 years – is one of my favorite groups I've ever been around," Nantz revealed. "That particular Wisconsin

team, whether you're talking about the national player of the year in Kaminsky, or Sam Dekker, or Nigel Hayes, or Gasser or Koenig or Traevon Jackson. There was something about them that was really fun and there was a magnetism about them.

"I know it's of little consolation to them, but they're going to always be remembered as the team that beat Kentucky. I just thought that as a team, that had no McDonald's All-Americans on its roster and almost won the national championship and beat a loaded team in Kentucky, I thought it was a powerful statement about college basketball. I think they really gave the game a jolt in the arm. To show people that you can win that way."

Following Monday night's championship game, the Badgers solemnly filed off the elevated Lucas Oil Stadium court amidst a backdrop of Duke-colored streamers and confetti. It's a shame many had their chins tucked into their chest as they departed the stage. Not only did these cardinal-clad heroes have no reason to hang their heads, but it also meant they likely missed a symbol that illustrated the impact of their glorious run.

Just above the tunnel as the Badgers exited was a sign with simple red letters that read:

Thanks Badgers
Made Us Believe

THE RUN THAT ALMOST WASN'T

"How do you want to feel on the bus ride home?"

That was the question Bo Ryan posed to his team on March 22, 2014 in the locker room at the BMO Harris Bradley Center in Milwaukee. The Badgers had just played one of their worst halves of the season and found themselves trailing Oregon, 49-37, in the 2014 NCAA Tournament Round of 32.

Everyone will remember Wisconsin's back-to-back Final Fours, but it is easy to forget that the Badgers were perilously close to not tasting any of that postseason sweetness. The magical run to North Texas in 2014, the Big Ten championships and dethroning of Kentucky in the 2015 Final Four can all be traced back to that nervous locker room in Milwaukee on March 22, 2014.

In order to understand how Wisconsin was still standing on the final day of the 2015 season, we must first look back. The Badgers' exhilarating comeback win over Oregon in 2014 will no doubt be remembered as a pivotal moment on the road to back-to-back Final Fours.

◆◆◆◆

Given a No. 2 seed, the Badgers were rewarded with a pair of "home" games just 90 miles east of Madison. After an incredibly thorough, 75-35, whitewashing of American in the opening round, Wisconsin had one more game at the Bradley Center before heading back to Madison. As the Badgers tangled with Oregon, the team's charter bus was packed and idling outside the arena, prepared to return the team home, regardless of the outcome.

"How do you want to feel on the bus ride home?"

Through the first 20 minutes, the team in white was almost unrecognizable. UW allowed the Ducks to shoot 56 percent from the field, surrendering a dizzying 19 fast break points. For a team that led the nation in fewest turnovers per game, the Badgers had coughed it up six times before intermission.

Things seemed to reach a boiling point in the final minute of the half when Ryan was whistled for a technical foul and the Oregon lead swelled to 14. The deficit was 12 as the Badgers retreated to a quiet and solemn locker room.

"Coach Ryan came into the locker room and told us about our mistakes and things we could correct, but also asked us, 'How do we want to feel?'" Josh Gasser explained. "Do we want this to be our last game? Do we want it to be our seniors' last game ever? That kind

Traevon Jackson jump-started the Badgers' 2014 rally vs. Oregon with an and-one to open the second half. *By Jeffrey Phelps*

Ben Brust left his mark on Wisconsin basketball as the school's all-time leader in 3-pointers, breaking the record with a pivotal shot vs. Oregon. *By Jeffrey Phelps*

of motivated us for the second half."

"You don't want to ever go down without at least putting yourself in a position to play your best," Ryan said. "I thought we left some things on the table in the first half that I knew our guys could do better."

In a game full of tide-changing plays, the first came on the opening possession of the second half. A Wisconsin airballed 3-pointer seemed like a cruel reminder of impending despair, but junior Traevon Jackson snuck in and grabbed a weakside rebound, finishing at the rim through a foul and earning a three-point play.

That put-back jumpstarted the floundering Badgers, but perhaps more importantly, invigorated the rabid, red-laden crowd of 18,206.

"The crowd was absolutely unbelievable in Milwaukee," Duje Dukan noted. "If it wasn't for them, I don't know if we would have made the run that we did."

That run came like a tidal wave. The Badgers scored 25 points in the first 7 minutes and 15 seconds, quickly erasing the deficit and setting the stage for a thrilling finish. Wisconsin was back in the game, and the only question that remained was would it be able to finish the job?

"Any time you have to come from behind," radio play-by-play voice Matt Lepay explained, "you wonder how much a team is going to have left in the tank after the energy that is expended to come back from a double-digit deficit and to take a game into the closing minutes."

With the Badgers trailing, 75-74, and 2:00 remaining, the tension in the Bradley Center was as thick as an Evan Anderson screen. Wisconsin would miss consecutive 3-point attempts, but offensive rebounds from Sam Dekker and Bronson Koenig kept the play

alive long enough for a hero to emerge – and enter the game.

"Down one, somebody needed to make a play," Gasser recalled. "I remember I took a 3 from the corner and thought it was going in. It didn't happen, but we got an offensive rebound and kicked it out. Trae (Jackson) took a shot that looked like it was going in, but it didn't happen and we ended up getting another offensive rebound and from there we took a timeout to regroup. We were kind of amped up, everyone wanted to make a play so badly."

Ryan's timeout not only settled the team down, but it also allowed him to reinsert

marksman Ben Brust into the game. Brust stepped back onto the floor with 227 career 3-pointers, one shy of the UW school record.

"I said, 'Ok let's get reorganized.' That's what a timeout is for," Ryan said. "And Ben is one of those guys that is always ready to come in and score."

Nineteen seconds – and yet another Dekker offensive rebound – after the timeout, Brust let a triple fly from the right wing... SWISH!

The long-range dagger made Brust Wisconsin's all-time 3-point king and gave the Badgers a lead they would never relinquish.

By David Stluka

"As soon as I let it fly, I knew it was in," Brust said after the game, unable to hold back a smile.

"I think it was the biggest 3 he ever made," Gasser noted. "If he doesn't make that, it might have been his last game ever. There were so many plays in that game that were huge, but that might have been the biggest."

"It was huge," Ryan conceded. "As people said, the Bradley Center was never as loud."

All five Badgers starters would score in double figures, with a team-high 19 from Frank Kaminsky and 16 from Jackson. UW hit 8-of-10 free throw attempts in the final 31 seconds to secure the win and send the "Kohl Center East" into absolute hysteria.

After the final buzzer had sounded, the Badgers joined a Badger Nation of 18,000-plus in a full-throated rendition of the school's alma mater, "Varsity," that reverberated from Sheboygan to Superior.

"That was the loudest arena I've played in, hands down," Dekker remembered fondly. "Our fans were so crazy that whole night. We definitely fed off it and it was a lot of fun. Singing 'Varsity' with that whole crowd was something I'll never forget."

"To be able to handle that smack in the face in the first half and come back and deliver one of our own says a lot about this group," Ryan said as his team prepared to move on to the Sweet 16 and beyond. ∎

I *CAN* BELIEVE I'M GOING TO SAY IT...

"That was just an emotional rollercoaster."

Wisconsin had not been to a Final Four since an improbable run in 2000 and before that, it had been 60 years since the Cardinal and White made an appearance in the national semifinals.

So if Bo Ryan and the Badgers were going to reach college basketball's final weekend, it was only fitting they would do so via one of the greatest games of the entire 2014 NCAA Tournament.

The Badgers would have to take down top-seeded Arizona, arguably the nation's top defensive team. UW would have to outlast overtime and endure one of the longest replay reviews on record. But in the same fashion the team used to bounce back from losing five of six games in January, it would take a stronger punch than that to knock Wisconsin to the canvas.

The Badgers entered the Elite Eight showdown off a clinical 69-52 dismantling of No. 6 seed Baylor. Perhaps the team's most thorough effort of the season was capped by a postgame locker room celebration with Packers MVP quarterback Aaron Rodgers.

Frank Kaminsky led UW with 19 points and six blocks as the Badgers took a Ginsu knife to Baylor's vaunted zone defense. At the other end, Wisconsin stifled a Bears offense that had blitzed third-seeded Creighton with an 85-55 rout one round earlier. Baylor matched its season-low point total while shooting a meager 32 percent.

Sam Dekker and the Badgers dismantled Baylor in the Sweet 16, setting the stage for a dramatic clash with Arizona.
By David Stluka

14

Frank Kaminsky's masterpiece against Arizona included 28 points and 11 rebounds. *By David Stluka*

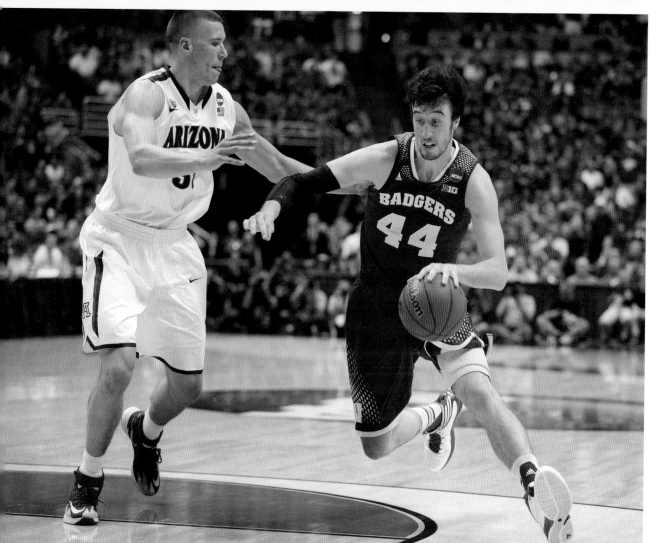

keep things close.

Frank Kaminsky had a modest eight points in the first half, but Turner Sports analyst Charles Barkley had seen enough to devise a second-half gameplan for the Badgers. During the TBS halftime show, Barkley stood in front of a chalkboard marked "Coaching With Chuck" and explained:

"The first thing I'm going to do is get the ball to Mr. Kaminsky. The second thing I'm going to do is get the ball to Mr. Kaminsky. The third thing? I'm going to get the ball to Mr. Kaminsky."

Bo Ryan and the Badgers took Sir Charles' advice.

Kaminsky scored three of Wisconsin's first four buckets of the second half including a 3-pointer that tied the game at 34-34, the first tie score since 0-0. The game would be a white-knuckler the rest of the way. In fact, the margin was never more than a one-possession game for the final 12:09 of regulation and the entire overtime period.

By the time Kaminsky was finished, he would turn in a virtuoso 28-point, 11-rebound performance that earned him West Regional Most Outstanding Player honors and the admiration of Arizona coach Sean Miller.

"Frank Kaminsky is the reason Wisconsin's in the Final Four," Miller said matter-of-factly after the game.

"I had a feeling going into the game," Kaminsky noted. "My shot was going in during warm-ups and I felt confident. Once my first 3 went in and I started making a few plays from the get go, I knew it could be a pretty good game. I kind of just kept building from there."

"Frank really carried us through the Arizona game," fellow All-West Regional Team selection Traevon Jackson added.

Arizona, meanwhile, came in armed with a 33-4 record and an impressive 23-point win over Gonzaga that preceded taking out San Diego State in the Sweet 16. The only No. 1 vs. No. 2 game in the tournament, this one had the makings of a classic.

Wisconsin and Arizona were pitted in a classic game of strength vs. strength. The Wildcats boasted the nation's No. 1 defense according to statistician Ken Pomeroy, while the same metric ranked the Badgers No. 4 offensively.

Much the way Wisconsin enjoyed its first two games in Milwaukee, Arizona was clearly the home favorite in Southern California.

"This was in essence a road game," Badgers play-by-play voice Matt Lepay explained. "There were a lot of Arizona fans. Anaheim to Tucson is a reachable distance."

It was clear from the onset that neither team would be able to pull away, matching each other shot for shot. Wisconsin trailed, 28-20, with 2:30 left in the half but scored the final five points before intermission to

"Everybody made big plays, but he really carried us. I just realized it with his expression and how he was playing, how free he was. We fed off that as a team."

Even with Kaminsky's heroics, the Badgers would need a pair of crucial defensive stops to punch their ticket to the Final Four.

Clinging to a 64-63 lead, Arizona's Nick Johnson was called for a push-off on a drive against Big Ten All-Defensive Team selection Josh Gasser with a mere 3.2 seconds left, giving the ball back to the Badgers. However, an in-bounds pass from Sam Dekker to Jackson deflected out of bounds in front of the Arizona bench. The play was too close to call, forcing the referees to huddle in front of a replay monitor for what seemed like an eternity.

"That was just an emotional rollercoaster," 2014 senior Ben Brust groaned. "Looking back, the replay was longer than any NFL replay I've ever seen in my life. But the time it took the refs to look at the replay and for as long as they did, I knew in my head, there was no way we were getting the ball back. So then we had to focus on what we were going to do defensively to get that stop."

The ball was originally ruled to Wisconsin, so the officials would need indisputable video evidence. Either way, in the Badgers huddle, Bo Ryan had already prepared for the call to be overturned and awarded to the Wildcats.

"What I talked about during that delay, in which I had a birthday it was so long," Ryan

Jae C. Hong

joked over the replay review that took nearly five minutes, "I started talking about 'Don't let anyone rim run off a backscreen, protect the rim; if they catch the ball, make them try to catch it going away from the basket.'"

As Ryan and the Badgers expected, the call was overturned and the ball went back to the Wildcats.

From a side out position, Pac-12 Player of the Year Nick Johnson caught the ball trailed by Gasser outside the 3-point arc. As he took a dribble to his left, Jackson jumped out to help defend, forcing Johnson to take two additional dribbles toward the opposite sideline, preventing him from getting a shot off before the buzzer sounded.

"I had a great view of the clock and the

guy shooting the ball," Brust said. "As soon as he put it on the floor I was thinking, 'he's not going to get that off.'"

Fourteen years earlier when the Badgers punched their improbable ticket to the 2000 Final Four, Lepay yelled his famous line about not believing what he was about to say. This time, the sentiment was much different.

On radios across the state of Wisconsin, Lepay's voice cracked as he roared, "I CAN believe I'm going to say it. Bo Ryan and the Wisconsin Badgers have punched their ticket to Texas. They're going to the Final Four."

"We saw that he missed and everybody just went nuts," Dukan beamed. "We finally realized that everything we had worked for and everything we had talked about in

On what would have been the 90th birthday of his father, Butch Ryan, Bo Ryan celebrated reaching his first Final Four. *By David Stluka*

remember being in awe of all the people back in Madison who were supporting us the whole time. I actually wanted to get back and celebrate with the fans just because they carried us for so long this season. Those are memories I'm going to look back on. It's hard not to crack a smile, it really is."

The party in the state capital would continue the next afternoon as the Badgers were welcomed home to the Kohl Center by more than 10,000 revelers still hoarse from the night before.

"I wish we could take this (trophy) and cut it into about 100,000 pieces and give one to every fan and all the people that supported us, people like you, who have helped make all this possible," Ryan boomed to the adoring sea of Badgers fans that filled all three decks of the arena. "It has been such a pleasure. Thank you very much for all you do and all your support. This is for you."

"To see what a couple games can do for some people was pretty special," Dekker would say looking back on the whirlwind weekend. "To come home to that was really eye-opening and made you appreciate how much these people make us better and make it well worth the effort it takes. To fill up the Kohl Center to see 16 guys walk into a gym is something I'll never forget." ∎

making it to a Final Four had finally come true."

"It was a feeling you can't describe as a basketball player," Dekker added. "It was shock, awe and just relief all in one."

What came next was a blur. As they had all tournament, the Badgers piled onto the back of Kaminsky who could do nothing but yell. There was Bo Ryan choking back tears in a postgame interview with TBS' Craig Sager as he remembered his father, Butch Ryan, who had passed away prior to the season.

Butch, who always reminded his son that he would reach the Final Four one day, would have turned 90 years old that day.

"I always look at the fans section where our people are because I did that at Platteville when we won our first national championship," Ryan reflected. "I looked at the people and the smiles and the hugs and the high fives and the fist pumps and everything else that takes place with the people who support you along the way."

Back in Madison a wild scene was unfolding as more than 10,000 people poured onto State Street chanting "Fi-nal Four! Fi-nal Four!"

"I remember in the locker room going on my phone and seeing all the videos from people on State Street," Kaminsky said. "I

BUTCH RYAN

"You'll get here next year, you'll see."

When Bo Ryan and the Badgers finally broke through and reached the 2014 national semifinals, it was by no means the first time the Ryan family had headlined a Final Four.

Ryan was hired as an assistant coach at Wisconsin in 1976 and attended his first Final Four as a member of college basketball's coaching fraternity. As fate would have it, that year's Final Four was held in Philadelphia, a mere top-of-the-arc 3-pointer from Ryan's hometown of Chester, Pa.

Ryan's father, Butch, made the short drive to join his son at the Spectrum, watching Indiana cap off an undefeated season with a win over Michigan in the 1976 national championship.

From then on, the Final Four became an annual bonding ritual for the duo. Butch would often drive an RV to the host city, a pile of Philly Cheesesteaks in tow. When Ryan became a Division I head coach, Butch was always the one building his spirits after another season ended short of his team reaching college basketball's Holy Grail.

"You'll get here next year, you'll see," Butch would say.

Even in 2013, when Butch was too ill to attend the Final Four games, Bo flew him to Atlanta anyway and the two watched from a hotel room.

38 years. Bo and Butch never missed a Final Four. Until 2014.

A pipefitter and decorated World War II

Bo Ryan coached the 2013-14 season with a heavy heart after losing his parents, Butch and Louise, prior to the season. *Courtesy of the Ryan Family*

veteran, Butch Ryan was quick with a joke and even quicker with giving his time to youth sports. A founding member of the Ashton (Pa.) Athletic Association, Butch dedicated his life to coaching area youth football, basketball and baseball. In 2011, the football field behind the Ashton Community Center was named Butch Ryan Field.

A larger-than-life personality, Butch was made for a bigger audience than Ashton. The Final Four provided that stage.

The stories are so legendary they almost seem unbelievable. However, if you ever met Butch Ryan, you know they are anything but a stretch. A member of the Final Four "All-Lobby" team 38 years running, Butch would spend equal time entertaining a crowd and

working the room for his son, who he called "Ace," to get his next job.

There was the time when Butch challenged MC Hammer to a dance-off in the Hilton lobby in New Orleans. Or the time he sang on stage with a trio of female singers and used the tip collection to buy the bar a round of Hurricanes at a different Final Four in New Orleans.

He once tied an orange UW-Platteville sweatshirt to the top of his RV so as not to be outdone by the other Division I team flags he saw flying high around town. Butch would

THROWN AROUND BY SMALL MEN WHO FIND IT EASIER TO LIVE IN THE WORLD THEY'VE BEEN GIVEN THAN TO EXPLORE THE POWER THEY HAVE TO CHANGE IT. IMPOSSIBLE IS NOT A FACT. IT'S AN OPINION ... T A DECLARATIO ... BLE IS POTENT ...

Never one to be shy, Butch Ryan danced his way to 38 Final Fours. *Courtesy of the Ryan Family*

sidestep security to brag up his son to legends like Dean Smith. At one Final Four, he laughed so hard he had to go to the hospital.

Butch Ryan became such a fixture at the Final Four that people would meet Bo and say, "Oh, you're Butch's son."

"More people knew my dad at Final Fours than me," Bo Ryan remembered. "It was our bonding time."

That's what made 2014 so bittersweet.

At the age of 89, Butch Ryan passed away on August 30, 2013. Two months before the Badgers would begin a season that would change the biography of his son.

On March 30, 2014 – the day Butch Ryan would have turned 90 years old – Wisconsin closed out a heart-stopping win over top-seeded Arizona, advancing to the Final Four. In a seemingly poetic injustice, Bo Ryan had finally captured his Great White Whale and Butch was not around to see it.

While his players embraced and donned shirts that read "Net Worthy," Ryan stopped for a postgame interview with Craig Sager of TBS. The candid moment peeled away the Chester-tough exterior and revealed the importance of Ryan's relationship with his best friend and father, Butch.

"It's going to be tough," Ryan choked. "It's going to be tough to be there coaching without him. But I can't imagine him being any happier, or my mom who passed away about a year ago.

"I'm happy. I'm happy that I've been able to be on the sideline and do this thing called coaching because my parents gave me the opportunity to pursue it. My wife, my kids, I can't thank them enough. These guys, a second family, you know how it is. But this is for Butch."

A sign at the Honda Center in Anaheim agreed; it read: "Final 4 Butch"

True to his father's teachings, after the game Ryan put the Badgers' first trip to the Final Four since 2000 into perspective.

"It's always about the players," Ryan said as he deflected the attention postgame. "It should always be about the players. My dad was always about the kids that he helped mentor growing up. That's why I do it.

"To be able to see the faces of these guys, to see the genuine excitement, I can remember some of the great teams that he had of kids, how they acted when they won their first championships and just had the joy. That's all I wanted to see."

That joy was what the UW players wanted to see for their coach as well.

Ben Brust, Josh Gasser, Frank Kaminsky and Zach Bohannon traveled to Chester in September of 2013 to represent the team at Butch Ryan's funeral and it was there that they gained an appreciation for Butch's legendary status and the depth of his relationship with his son.

"We learned how close Coach is with his family," Kaminsky revealed. "He had a lot of similarities with how he grew up and how he coaches. His life wasn't always easy. He had family members that were tough on him and expected the best out of him. But he wanted to prove himself to his parents and especially his dad. That's the way a lot of us are on the team. Coach wants the best for us like his dad wanted for him.

"We wanted the Final Four for Coach Ryan, just like he wanted it for us."

"You knew the Final Four was something Coach would do with his dad every year and it was very special to them," Brust explained. "It's really meaningful to be the first team to help Coach Ryan reach the Final Four. To be able to get there in the year that Butch died, it was almost a storybook ending."

As the wild postgame celebration unfolded, the Badgers players formed a ring on the court, taking turns dancing and reveling in the moment. Before dispersing and making their way to the ladder awaiting the team's net cutting, the middle of the circle went empty. The players continued dancing to no particular music, filled with an unmistakable spirit.

Perhaps that was Butch's turn to dance.

Bo certainly believed he was there.

"When I was asked about my dad, it was his birthday. It would have been his 90th birthday," Ryan would say later. "I certainly wish he could have been there physically, but in spirit is good enough for me. My mother having passed away eight months before, I think both of them were smiling."

Smiling, and no doubt dancing. ∎

KENTUCKY BLUES

"Now get ready, because they say things are big in Texas."

When the celebration from knocking off Arizona to advance to the 2014 Final Four in Dallas had subsided, Bo Ryan stood in front of his team in the Badgers' Anaheim, Calif., locker room. His jacket still damp from the postgame shower his players had given him, Ryan commanded the team's attention.

"You've earned the right to 40 more minutes. Thanks for taking me with you. Now get ready, because they say things are big in Texas."

He couldn't have been more right. From the blockbuster movie set built for the team's promotional shoot to the grandiose AT&T Stadium, it was clear Wisconsin Basketball had moved to a big time stage.

The team's first look at the home of the Dallas Cowboys was during its closed practice on Thursday afternoon. Emerging from the tunnel into the football-stadium-turned-world's-largest-arena, many of the Badgers were speechless, with grins as wide as the 180-foot video board which dwarfed the court below.

"Wow," was all Duje Dukan could utter. "It feels like we're outside," Sam Dekker giggled.

"As we came through the tunnel and looked out, I thought, 'Oh my goodness,'" said Ryan, still in reverence months later. "Huge doesn't describe it. Gigantic isn't good enough. Awesome. That's the only word I can use, because that's how it hit me. This is unbelievable."

"I remember my friends telling me that they were up in the fourth deck and they got free binoculars for sitting that far away," Kaminsky chuckled. "That's just kind of a mind-blowing thing for a basketball game."

In front of a crowd of 79,444, the largest ever to witness a college basketball game, Wisconsin and Kentucky would stage one of the greatest national semifinals in recent memory.

Kentucky, which began the season as the No. 1 team in the 2014 Associated Press preseason poll, had rediscovered itself after stumbling to a No. 8 seed in the Big Dance. But the Badgers were surging as well and held a lead for the final 15 minutes of the first half.

In a half that featured a combined nine minutes played from Traevon Jackson and Nigel Hayes due to foul trouble, Bronson Koenig emerged as an early hero. The freshman from La Crosse hadn't scored more than five points in any of Wisconsin's NCAA tournament games but showed no fear at the Final Four, outscoring each of Kentucky's vaunted freshmen with 11 first-half points.

The Badgers' 40-36 halftime lead quickly evaporated as Kentucky sprinted ahead, 51-43, in the first five minutes of the second half. The Wildcats scored 10 of their 46 points in the paint during that stretch as UW had trouble with the imposing UK front line.

Wisconsin would use a spark from another reserve, this time Dukan, to answer with a 10-2

▶ Wisconsin's 2014 matchup with Kentucky was witnessed by a crowd of 79,444 people, the largest ever for a college basketball game. *By David Stluka*

Kentucky's Aaron Harrison sank the Badgers with this deep 3-pointer, but provided the motivation Wisconsin would carry until the two would meet again. *By David Stluka*

By David J. Phillip

run and even the score at 53-all. The final 12:00 would feature a series of ties and lead changes, setting up a heart-stopping finish.

With the score tied at 71-71 and 16.4 seconds remaining, savvy veteran Traevon Jackson drew a three-shot foul when his defender left his feet on a shot fake from the top of the arc. Jackson would hit two of three at the line, the miss counting for Wisconsin's only missed free throw of the game (19-of-20), to push the Badgers ahead by two.

At the other end of the floor Kentucky freshman Aaron Harrison would make a play that would stain the Badgers' memory for eternity. Similar to a shot he made the previous weekend in the regional final to beat Michigan, Harrison drained an NBA-range 3-pointer over an outstretched Josh Gasser to put the Wildcats ahead 74-73 with just 5.7 seconds left to play.

The Badgers would get off one final shot, but as Jackson's pull-up jumper from the left elbow rimmed out, the magical 2014 season had come to a screeching halt.

Stunned silence gave way to tears and hugs in the Wisconsin locker room. The fact that several national media members remarked it was the most emotional locker room they'd ever been in illustrated the agony of such a brutal loss, as well as the once-in-a-generation bond this team had created.

None of the players in that locker room knew if they'd ever experience another Final Four, but they all knew that the path to the Promised Land had been outlined and the hunger to return would only grow stronger.

"It really gave us hope for the next year. We made it," Jackson said after the season, pausing before continuing. "But we can do that again. It didn't finish the way we wanted it to, but it left us with hope to do it again."

That summer when Ryan sat down for an interview reflecting on the season, he offered the following prophetic words:

"One more basket and we would have been playing for a national championship. That was something I know these guys will never forget.

"You never know what the future holds. There are teams that have done that and then never get the magic back. Then there are teams that have done it and the magic returns. Hopefully we're one of those teams that can make some more good things happen."

Good things indeed. ∎

GREAT EXPECTATIONS

"Nothing is going to stop us."

This much is true: Wisconsin's historic 2014-15 season could not have happened without the crushing ending of the previous year.

The Badgers' last-second loss to Kentucky in the 2014 Final Four served as a humbling reminder that success can be fleeting. By the time Wisconsin returned home from Texas on April 7, devastation and anguish had already given way to determination and anger.

"This should make people pissed off and hungry going into next season, this offseason," Frank Kaminsky seethed minutes after the 2014 national semifinal. "We've got a lot to do. We saw what we needed to do in the postseason to get here. We'll take that going forward and build on what we've accomplished this season. We want to be back here next year, and win a championship next year. We know we can be contenders, and nothing is going to stop us."

The sour taste from the Aaron Harrison dagger in Dallas was still on the lips of the team as they reassembled in June.

"That loss to Kentucky affected us a lot going into the offseason," Gasser acknowledged. "You wanted to get back to work immediately. We were so motivated to get in the gym and in the weight room and work hard. That loss was heart-breaking, but it allowed the next year's success to happen."

Wisconsin would be losing only senior starter Ben Brust and reserves Evan Anderson and Zach Bohannon, while returning seven of the top eight scorers from the previous season. That collective backbone made the Badgers a unanimous pick to win the Big Ten in 2015 and placed them on a preseason short list of national title contenders.

Expectations had never been higher for the University of Wisconsin. Expectations that could wilt the weak or fracture the feeble.

Not this team, not this year.

"We never shied away from expectations," Sam Dekker admitted. "I'd be lying if I told you we didn't pay attention to that stuff. We heard it all and knew where we were ranked and everything. But I guarantee nobody had higher expectations for us than the guys in our own locker room."

Where a Big Ten championship and Final Four were team *goals* in 2014, they were now *expectations* in 2015. The national championship was the team goal.

"We knew we had something special," Kaminsky said without a hint of arrogance. "We believed in ourselves and we believed that we were the best team in the country and we had the opportunity to go out there and do it. It just felt right, so why not talk about it. It was a feeling that everyone had, so we just kind of validated it by acknowledging it."

"In all of my years here it was always our goal to win a Big Ten championship and make a Final Four," Gasser furthered. "We always knew we could do it, but we didn't truly believe we were going to. Making the 2014 Final Four gave us so much confidence that we are good enough and we will get back to that point."

So singular was the team's focus on winning championships in 2015 that the idea of raising the 2014 Final Four banner prior to the season opener wasn't even fully embraced.

▶ **The Badgers raised a Final Four banner prior to the 2015 season opener, but their eyes were already on what lied ahead, not what was behind.** *By David Stluka*

"I don't know if I really want to," Kaminsky replied when asked to pull the cord that would unfurl the Kohl Center addition prior to the November season opener. "I mean, I'm proud of 2014 and the banner and everything, but right now I don't really want to look back at what we did last year. I want to look forward to this year's mission, what we want to accomplish moving forward."

Never one to boast about specific ambitions, in this instance, Bo Ryan was in lock step with his team from day one of summer instruction.

"I told them I would go along with them, I would patrol the sidelines, I'm with you," Ryan would retell. "But I don't ever put that on teams, 'Hey, you've got to do this or you're not fulfilling expectations.' It's more, 'OK guys, you ready? Let's go. Roll your sleeves up, let's get after it.'"

For the Badgers, getting after it in the summer meant individual success leading to collective success. Under the guidance of second-year strength and conditioning coach Erik Helland, the players never lost focus of how their daily efforts fit into the greater picture.

"I think when you look at the journey, it's an evolution not a revolution," said Helland, a 25-year veteran of the NBA who joined the Badgers in June of 2013. "Someone who radically changes what they were doing probably wasn't doing things all that right in the first place. From the first day I met this team throughout the end of the two years, I saw a linear evolution of who they are and how they do their business on a daily basis.

"That first season was more about believing in yourself and believing you can compete at that level and understanding what needs to be done in terms of how we prepare – in the weight room, on the track, in the training room, on the court. All of

those things are seamlessly intertwined. As the quality of what we do improves, our outcomes improve along with it."

"Erik was huge for us. He knew what it took to be a champion, because he saw it so many times with the Bulls," Kaminsky said, referencing Helland's six NBA championship rings. "He knew how you had to prepare and conduct yourself and how you had to treat your body and get right before every game. You have to treat every day like it was a championship that day. That's the mindset he instilled in us from the day he got here."

"The first year was very much about believing in ourselves and the second year was about raising the bar and embracing that challenge that came with it," added Helland.

That summer Ryan sat in the bleachers of an AAU tournament in South Carolina scouring the prep talent and talking with *Sports Illustrated* writer Seth Davis. When the topic turned to expectations, Ryan offered a simple response.

"I like the respect people have shown to our guys. That, to me, is rewarding," Ryan told Davis. "The only thing that matters is how much better we can be. If my guys stay coachable, keep their minds, ears and eyes open, I think we can be OK." ∎

▲ "Erik Helland was huge for us. He knew what it took to be a champion." – Frank Kaminsky *By Patrick Herb*

▶ Frank Kaminsky decided to return to Wisconsin for his senior season in part to get an even bigger ring than the team earned in 2014.
By John Fisher | Cal Sport Media

THE BATTLE 4 ATLANTIS

"We wanted to win every possible thing."

Wisconsin's 2014-15 season began with little resistance, the Badgers rolling through their first four non-conference games, winning by an average margin of 28 points. In back-to-back games, the Badgers posted 24-point wins over future postseason participants Boise State and Green Bay. It was clear from the start that UW's preseason No. 3 ranking was deserved.

It was also evident that preseason All-American Frank Kaminsky was living up to the hype, posting double-doubles in each of UW's first three games before a dominating 26-point performance against Boise State in game four. Kaminsky was a remarkable 11-for-13 from the field, including 4-for-5 from 3-point range. This was indeed going to be a special season for the Badgers big man.

Prior to the season, the Badgers had very clear goals and expectations. As they departed for the Bahamas on November 24, the players had one thing on their minds.

"We wanted to win every possible thing we could win," Josh Gasser said, boiling it down to the simplest terms. "The Battle 4 Atlantis was our first goal and we treated it like it was our first championship. The field was as good as an Elite Eight. Pretty much every team down there had a great season and did well in the NCAA tournament."

To Gasser's point, seven of the eight teams in the 2014 Battle 4 Atlantis would ultimately be selected for the NCAA tournament. In fact, all seven won their first game in the Big Dance with four (Wisconsin, North Carolina, Oklahoma and UCLA) reaching the Sweet 16. Interestingly, preseason No. 7 Florida was the

The Badgers flew to the Bahamas seeking their first of five potential championships on the season.
Top and Right photos: *By Patrick Herb*

only team from Atlantis not to make March Madness.

"We knew going into it that it was a great field," Sam Dekker explained. "We were really looking forward to it because we had heard how cool Atlantis was but it was also a great opportunity to see how we stacked up against some of best teams in the country early on."

Setting the scene, the Battle 4 Atlantis tournament is held in the Imperial Ballroom of the Atlantis resort on appropriately-named Paradise Island, Bahamas. The unique setting featured a low ceiling, complete with chandeliers. The court was illuminated brightly, but the temporary bleachers on the edges were cloaked in a blue darkness that made it feel like the teams were playing on a

strange underwater stage.

The eight-team, three-game tournament was also played against a backdrop of water slides, pristine beaches, shark pools and even a casino that teams walked through on their way to and from every game. To say there were distractions would be an understatement.

It was in Atlantis that the Badgers first demonstrated their incredible ability to separate fun and focus. Mere minutes after arriving at the resort you could find the entire team, all 15 of them, alternating trips down the giant water slides and splashing in the ocean or playing touch football on the beach.

"One of the neat things about the Bahamas trip that was reflective of the entire season was that when we did something, we did it together," Dekker revealed. "There were no cliques on the team. We had one group message chain that included the entire team. If you wanted to get something out, it went to the whole team. So if someone had an idea, we were all in on it. That was the most fun trip we've taken because there was a healthy balance of basketball and fun. Everybody did everything together."

"That first night we were there was really fun," Zak Showalter said. "The whole team was just chilling by the beach. We just played. I remember burying Nigel up to his

head in the sand and tossing each other into the ocean. When you live in Wisconsin, it is pretty hard to beat 80 degrees in late November."

But after top-seeded Wisconsin rolled past UAB, 72-43, in the opener Kaminsky assured the media that the Badgers were focused on their assignment.

"We're having a great time here, but as fun as Atlantis is with all the water slides and everything, this is a business trip for us."

Kaminsky led the way for the Badgers with 16 points against a struggling UAB team that would lose all three games in the Bahamas and begin the season just 2-5. Nobody would have guessed that team would later rally to make the NCAA tournament and stun No. 3 seed Iowa State in the opening round.

Things would get tougher for the Badgers in the second round on Thanksgiving Day against a Georgetown team that had just posted an impressive overtime win over Florida the night before. At that point in the season, Wisconsin had not trailed in the second half of a game, but that changed when the Hoyas built a nine-point lead, 53-44, with 11:30 remaining. The Badgers were having a difficult time containing Georgetown's inside-outside threat of guard D'Vauntes Smith-Rivera and 6-foot-10, 350-pound center Joshua Smith.

"Georgetown was a physical and

Despite only six points from Frank Kaminsky, Wisconsin erased a nine-point second-half deficit against Georgetown and advanced to the Battle 4 Atlantis championship game. By AP Photo

By AP Photo

Dukan scored eight consecutive points for the Badgers, giving them their first lead since the opening minutes of the half.

"When Trae and I got in foul trouble, Coach Ryan didn't put us back in until about one minute left because we told him to keep the other guys out there," Gasser acknowledged. "Usually we'd go back in with three or four minutes left but when we went on our run, Duje and Bronson were out there and doing well. Coach asked us if we were ready to check in and we both said to leave them in. That was kind of a coming out party for those two and helped our depth moving forward."

Koenig tied his then-career high with 14 points and Dukan added eight, including a pair of pivotal 3-pointers. For the three-game tournament, Dukan averaged 27 minutes and 10.6 points per game while knocking down 6 of his 11 3-point attempts, inspiring *Sports Illustrated's* Seth Davis to pen from courtside:

"Just what the Badgers needed to find out: They have yet another big man who can shoot from deep."

At 6-foot-9 and 220 pounds, senior forward Duje Dukan is ready to step into the pantheon of Bo Ryan players who developed slowly, waited their turn and then took advantage when the opportunity to play presented itself."

tough team, maybe along the lines of Michigan State," Hayes remembered. "Their big guy, Josh Smith, might be the largest player we'll ever play against in our lives. They gave us a challenge."

Wisconsin was still trailing at the under-8:00 timeout and starting guards Traevon Jackson and Josh Gasser were both on the bench saddled with four fouls. That's when Bo Ryan employed the team's "Redwoods" lineup, consisting of four players 6-foot-8 or taller along with one guard. In this case, Kaminsky, Dekker, Hayes and Duje Dukan joined Bronson Koenig.

The Redwoods, and Dukan in particular, would give Wisconsin a shot in the arm.

▲ **Wisconsin's championship win over Oklahoma was one of 18 on the season over teams that would make up the 2015 NCAA Tournament field.** *By Patrick Herb*

◄ **"The first night we were there was really fun. The whole team was just chilling by the beach. We just played. I remember burying Nigel Hayes up to his head in the sand and tossing each other into the ocean." – Zak Showalter** *By Patrick Herb*

The game was still very much in doubt with 2:30 remaining and the Badgers ahead, 64-59. During a timeout Ryan commanded his players' attention sensing the tense feeling in the ballroom/arena.

"Listen up," Ryan barked, trying to be heard over the Georgetown crowd's chant of "Ho-ya, Sax-a, Ho-ya, Sax-a."

"Can you hear that?" Ryan asked, pretending to listen to the crowd.

"Coach was all serious and we thought he was about to yell at us for something," Hayes explained. "But instead, he started chanting 'Re-bound, re-bound, re-bound,' along with the crowd. We all just started laughing and it really relaxed us. Then we went out there and won the game, a big game."

The Badgers would indeed win the game, but it took an acrobatic tip-in from Hayes with 20 seconds remaining and a missed 3-pointer from Smith-Rivera at the buzzer to pull it out. Smith-Rivera had 29 points and was 5-for-5 from behind the arc until that last shot, but Wisconsin double-teamed him with Jackson and Kaminsky on the final possession and forced the clinching miss.

"That tournament was a nice confidence booster for me," Dukan said looking back. "I

had missed the first two games of the season after that strange eligibility issue from playing in the exhibition games two years before when I had mono, so the Battle 4 Atlantis kind of jump-started the season for me."

"I'm proud of Duje," Gasser offered. "The fact that he stuck it out over his career and was unselfish enough to just want to be a Badger and be part of winning teams. He could have transferred somewhere and averaged 15-20 points per game at a smaller conference team that may not win as many games, but he wanted to contribute and play at the highest level. He wanted to play for championships. Guys like that are what make a team great."

In the championship game, the Badgers faced an Oklahoma team that had posted double-digit wins over UCLA and Butler to reach the title game.

When Kaminsky picked up his second foul just five and a half minutes in, Wisconsin's depth was put to a test in the championship game as well. The eventual tournament MVP would not return the rest of the half. As the old adage goes, next man up.

"A lot of teams might have gotten rattled when their star player goes down like Frank did with his foul trouble," Hayes said. "But the type of team we had, whenever a guy wasn't having a great game or went down, his teammates picked him up."

Again it was Dukan picking up the slack, hitting a trio of 3s and scoring 11 points in a first half that featured 11 lead changes. Wisconsin clung to a 34-33 lead at intermission.

"I was frustrated at halftime," Kaminsky admitted. "I hadn't been in foul trouble much at all in my career and I hated sitting on the bench that whole half and not being able to help my teammates. They did a great job of keeping us in it, and I knew I needed to be

Reserve Duje Dukan provided a big lift for UW at the Battle 4 Atlantis, including 13 points against Oklahoma in the title game. *By Patrick Herb*

the best player I could be in that second half."

Kaminsky and Wisconsin would answer the call in the second half. The Badgers scored 16 of the first 18 points after halftime, sprinting to a 50-35 lead. UW also clamped down on defense, forcing 21 Oklahoma turnovers and limiting the Sooners to 2-for-14 shooting over a 10-minute stretch that overlapped halftime. OU would never get closer than nine points the rest of the way as Kaminsky scored 14 of his 17 points in the final 20 minutes and finished as one of five Badgers in double figures.

As "Jump Around" blared over the ballroom speakers, the Badgers donned Battle 4 Atlantis champion hats and shirts and paraded their conch-shelled trophy around the pro-Wisconsin crowd.

"Our fans were crazy down there like always," Gasser laughed when thinking back. "It was such a long walk from the court back to our hotel rooms and we would always get stopped a hundred times for pictures and autographs. I remember after the championship game we wanted to rush back to our rooms so we all gathered in one tight line and hung onto the shoulders of the guy in front of you and sprinted through everyone. We must have looked ridiculous yelling and running through the casino and lobby, but it was the only way we'd be able to get through without being mobbed. The fans were awesome, but it was hilarious."

Three quality wins in three days and the Badgers had checked the first championship off their wish list.

"Winning the Battle 4 Atlantis was sweet," Dekker mused. "That was during a time when I wasn't playing as many minutes because of my ankle injury and it gave me a chance to watch guys step up, guys like Nigel, Bronson, Duje, Showy. That was our first championship of the year and made a statement early because it was a great bracket. We made a point to celebrate and appreciate that one." ▪

By Patrick Herb

A BREAK IN MOMENTUM

"Be the hunter instead of the hunted."

January 11 served as a turning point in the Badgers' 2014-15 season. Save for a loss to Duke in the Big Ten/ACC Challenge, Wisconsin had seemed nearly untouchable.

UW was 15-1, with those wins coming by an average of 22.1 points per game. The Badgers had spent the entire season in the top six of the AP poll and had no doubt developed a swagger.

"We were really confident heading into the season, but the way we were beating teams early really made us feel pretty comfortable," junior Sam Dekker explained. "I wouldn't say that trip to Rutgers was a wake-up call, but maybe a reminder that we're not invincible. It reinforced that we needed to be the aggressor, be the hunter instead of the hunted."

The first sign of UW's vulnerability came four days prior in a hard-fought 62-55 win over Purdue at the Kohl Center. The Boilermakers entered the game as a heavy underdog after head-scratching December losses to Gardner-Webb and North Florida. However, when Purdue led 19-14 midway through the first half, it was clear the hard-nosed Boilermakers, the team that had beaten eventual NCAA tournament teams NC State and BYU around Thanksgiving, had returned.

Purdue would hang tough, tying the game at 45-45 with 6:25 remaining, but the Badgers answered with a 9-2 run to seize control and exit with a victory.

"It was good to grind out a win like this, low-scoring," Josh Gasser would say, referring to the fact UW had scored 80-plus points in each of its previous two Big Ten games. "We had to fight the

The Badgers moved to 15-1 with a win over Purdue, but it came at a price, as Frank Kaminsky suffered a concussion that would keep him out of the team's next game at Rutgers. *By David Stluka*

Josh Gasser scored a season-high 15 points in the 62-55 win over the Boilermakers. **By John Fisher | Cal Sport Media**

adversity, stay mentally tough. That's what we needed."

A trademark of the season, Wisconsin benefited from a huge disparity at the free throw line, going 25-for-31 at the stripe while Purdue was just 3-for-7. The game also served as Bo Ryan's 159th career Big Ten win, surpassing Hall of Famer Walter Meanwell for the most in school history.

Frank Kaminsky led the Badgers with 21 points (11-for-14 at the free throw line) and

Gasser contributed a season-high 15 points. But the win would come at a price.

During the first half, Kaminsky was on the wrong end of an inadvertent elbow from Purdue's 7-foot-2, 297-pound mountain of a man, freshman Isaac Haas. Kaminsky would finish the game but later developed dizziness, fatigue and light sensitivity, raising concern from UW's sports medicine staff. Kaminsky was diagnosed with a concussion, putting his status for the

Badgers' next game at Rutgers in jeopardy.

A game-time decision, Kaminsky was ultimately ruled out. His absence marked the end of a remarkable streak. It had been over two years – exactly 77 games – since a Badgers starter had missed a game due to injury. In an era of heightened attention and precaution over head trauma, no one could blame the school's medical team for looking out for Kaminsky.

Well, no one except Kaminsky, that is.

"I didn't practice those next few days but I still went on the trip and hoped I'd be cleared by the time we played," Kaminsky said. "By the time gameday rolled around I felt fine and really wanted to play. In fact, I was on the phone that day with one of our team doctors back in Madison lobbying to be cleared. I guess I'm not a very good negotiator. At the time I was upset with the decision, but now I understand why they did it and I'm thankful that Henry (Perez-Guerra), our trainer, and our medical team is there to protect us from ourselves sometimes."

There was no one there to protect Wisconsin from what would happen next.

Wisconsin appeared to handle the lineup adjustment without Kaminsky just fine, cruising to a 12-point halftime lead thanks to 47 percent shooting and 10 points from Dekker. But a steal and breakaway dunk from Rutgers senior Kadeem Jack gave the Scarlet Knights life early in the second half. Rutgers erased the deficit and drew even at 46-46 with 12:19 remaining on a rainbow 3-pointer from Myles Mack in front of the Rutgers bench.

Things went from bad to worse for the Badgers as senior Traevon Jackson came down on Mack's foot while attempting to close out on the shooter. Jackson collapsed in agony and later limped off the court and into the bowels of the Rutgers Athletic Center. The severity of Jackson's foot injury would not be known for a few days, but the gravity of the loss was felt instantly.

Now down two starters, UW simply could not stem the big red tide. Rutgers shot 67 percent in the second half and outscored the Badgers 44-27 over the game's final 20 minutes to pull off one of the most inexplicable and improbable upsets of the entire college basketball season.

Rutgers would win a total of two games in its inaugural season in the Big Ten, but now had one that left head coach Eddie Jordan in tears.

"It's a great win for the program," Jordan said after what some considered the biggest win in Rutgers history. "I'm happy for our community."

While the home locker room relished in a timid court rush, the tenor was much different in the solemn Wisconsin locker room.

Slumped in the cramped and antiquated visiting locker room, no one knew what to say.

"Frank or no Frank, Trae or no Trae, we still should have won that game," senior Duje Dukan angrily muttered to no one in particular.

With Frank Kaminsky helplessly looking on from the bench, Bo Ryan could hardly watch the Badgers' second-half lead slip away at Rutgers.
By Cal Sport Media

"What just happened?" Gasser asked rhetorically.

Largely it was silence that filled the room. After 5 minutes that seemed like 50, Gasser and Kaminsky brought the team to its feet and delivered a message that would resonate far beyond those cinder block walls.

"It sucks to lose," Gasser barked. "I hate losing. But we've just got to have a short memory. One loss won't define who we are."

"We learned last year that one game can turn into more than one game," Kaminsky added with the memory of UW's five losses in six games a year prior still in his mind. "We had a (bad) loss. We've got to learn from it, we've got to move on from it. We can't live in the past. We can take a lot from this and use it going forward, but don't for a second hang your heads and let this affect anything other than tonight."

The Badgers had certainly learned their lesson. It would be six weeks before they lost again. ∎

Sam Dekker (left) led UW with 15 points against the Scarlet Knights, but an apparent foot injury suffered by Traevon Jackson (below) cast a cloud over the road trip. *By Cal Sport Media*

FROM BAD TO WORSE

"Trae is so mentally tough, it rubs off on the entire team."

The day after a stunning loss at Rutgers, Wisconsin's sports medicine staff confirmed what everyone feared. Senior point guard Traevon Jackson had fractured a bone in his right foot when he landed on the foot of Scarlet Knights guard Myles Mack. Jackson would miss significant time.

Subsequent surgery on January 15 left the Badgers without one of their senior leaders indefinitely. The hole was gaping.

Jackson had played in 106 games, starting the last 83 straight. UW's fourth-leading scorer (9.5 points per game) and top assist man at the time, statistics were only a small measure of Jackson's impact on the Badgers.

"The thing people don't know about Trae is how much he cared about our team and how much he wanted every single person to be involved and be playing the best basketball that they could be playing," Frank Kaminsky explained. "He's great at motivating people and telling people when they needed to pick it up or when they needed to calm down. He was just a really good floor leader. He read situations well. Sometimes he took a lot of criticism for certain things he was doing out on the court, but a lot of the time it was his doing when others were doing well because he put them in those situations to be successful."

"Trae is so mentally tough," Sam Dekker said. "When you have a point guard like that, it rubs off on the entire team."

"He was really good at instilling confidence in the other guys on the court and telling everyone to be aggressive at all times," fellow senior Josh Gasser noted. "Every time he passed it to you, he would be like, 'Shoot it, shoot it.' He wanted you to shoot with confidence.

"If someone made a shot, he'd run a play to get it right back to them the next time down. Or I can remember games where me or Sam or somebody maybe weren't that involved in the offense or getting shots and he'd say, 'Alright we need to run a play for you to get you going.' It worked both ways; if

Traevon Jackson played in 111 games for Wisconsin, but a broken right foot at Rutgers kept him out of the Badgers lineup for 19 games during his senior season.
By John Fisher | Cal Sport Media

The son of legendary Ohio State alum Jim Jackson, Traevon made a name for himself at Wisconsin, finishing with more than 800 points and 300 assists. *By John Fisher | Cal Sport Media*

somebody was hot, he'd want to get the ball to him every time. Or if somebody wasn't as involved he would try to get them going. He did a great job of spreading the wealth and keeping everyone confident."

Funny that instilling confidence was one of Jackson's greatest strengths because that was an area in which he himself needed an assist.

A lightly-recruited guard with legendary bloodlines, Jackson was eager to get out of the shadow of his father, All-American and 14-year NBA veteran, Jim Jackson. Traevon wasn't recruited by his father's alma mater, Ohio State. But that was OK with him. Raised largely by his mother, Tamara Winston, "Trae" wanted to make a name for himself.

Jackson picked UW over Arizona State and Dayton and came to Madison as a defense-first, offensive work in progress. Putting in the work wasn't the issue, opportunity was.

Unquestionably one of the hardest workers on the team, Jackson routinely stayed long after practice working by himself on ball-handling, shooting, flexibility, anything to improve. He played in just 17 games, averaging 5.4 minutes per game as a freshman and admitted that the frustration got to him.

Even after he earned the starting point guard spot early in his sophomore season, Jackson battled anger, often serving as a lightning rod for more criticism than he deserved.

"The negativity would manifest itself to the point where honestly I didn't even want to play," Jackson admitted in a 2014 story by FoxSportsWisconsin.com. "I questioned it a lot. I questioned it because I got to the point where I didn't love the game anymore."

Things would change for Jackson in the summer of 2013 while training near his home in Westerville, Ohio, with Anthony Rhodman, who founded In God's Image Sports Training. Putting in nearly seven hours a day, five days a week, Jackson immersed himself in a combination of basketball and spiritual guidance that he proudly acknowledges changed his life.

A new Jackson returned to Madison before the 2013-14 season.

"Trae came back a different person, in a good way," Dekker said at the time. "He was always a good person, but maybe now he's more humble and gracious and a better teammate. He openly talks about how blessed he is to be in this situation. He's bold about his faith and not afraid to be himself. I respect that."

Jackson was a different player on the court as well. He averaged 10.7 points, leading the Badgers in free throws and earning All-West Region honors during the 2014 NCAA Tournament. In 2015, Jackson was off to a strong start, having increased his field goal percentage and decreased his turnovers. Then the injury struck.

Jackson would be sidelined for a minimum of six weeks and the uncertainty of what laid ahead was measurable.

"After the Rutgers game I was really down," Gasser said. "I don't want to say our season was in jeopardy, but my confidence in our team was shaken. I knew our depth was going to be a struggle and Trae was such a good leader on the court. Obviously he was a good player, and Bronson (Koenig) is a really good player too, but I knew it was the intangibles that would be tough to replace." ∎

CHANGING OF THE GUARD

"No fear, no doubt, just go out there and play free."

Back in Madison with the sting of UW's 67-62 loss at Rutgers two days earlier beginning to fade, sophomore guard Bronson Koenig sat alone in his apartment, his mind whirring. That evening, Koenig had finished his first practice as the newly minted starting point guard at Wisconsin, an appointment the La Crosse, Wis., native had dreamed of since he first watched Devin Harris lead the Badgers to a Big Ten championship in 2003.

Koenig always knew he'd take the starting reins one day, but didn't expect it to be at the expense of his teammate and locker room neighbor. The day before, an X-ray and MRI had confirmed that Traevon Jackson had a broken foot and would be sidelined indefinitely.

As Koenig laid in bed at his off-campus apartment, he was conflicted. Filled with excitement about the opportunity, but stricken with guilt over a fallen brother, Koenig tapped out a text message to Jackson.

Hey bro, hope you're doing alright. I'm really sorry to hear about your foot. You know I'll pray for you. You've taught me so much this past year and a half and I am thankful for that. Whether it be basketball or just life in general which you don't even realize you've taught me. I hope you'll be able to continue to help me on and off the court, especially since you took over your soph year too. Appreciate it man

By Chris Steppig

As a freshman, Bronson Koenig showed flashes of his brilliance, highlighted by scoring 11 first-half points in the 2014 Final Four matchup vs. Kentucky.
By David Stluka

their programs when they came to watch his older teammates like Sam Dekker and J.P. Tokoto, a Menomonee Falls, Wis., native who would go on to play at the University of North Carolina.

"Bronson is a young man who, when he was playing up there in La Crosse and going to AAU stuff and going to Catholic League tournaments, his name was abuzz around the state," Bo Ryan said. "A lot of people knew about Bronson."

Koenig's legend only grew when he led La Crosse Aquinas to the Wisconsin high school state championship as a sophomore and again as a senior. A major coup for the Badgers, Koenig rose to a top-100 recruit and committed to UW over a list that included college basketball's elite.

"He's worked extremely hard to put himself into position to have a lot of options nationally on where to go to school," Ryan said on signing day in 2012, his first public comments about Koenig. "We're elated that he's chosen to stay home and play for the Badgers. I know our fans will really enjoy watching him grow, develop and help lead our teams in the future."

How prophetic Ryan was.

Koenig played in all but one game as a freshman, averaging 15.5 minutes in a reserve role. He showed flashes of what was to come, like his 12-point effort at Iowa or going 4-for-4 from 3-point range in UW's runaway win over Minnesota in the 2014 Big Ten Tournament. But it was on the grandest stage that Koenig announced he was ready for the spotlight.

In front of nearly 80,000 people at AT&T Stadium and millions more on television, Koenig dazzled in the first half of

A few hours later, at 12:23 a.m., Koenig's phone lit up with the following response from his elder backcourt mate.

Of course bro, always gonna be here for you regardless of the game, life has way more to it than strictly ball. Thanks for sharing that with me though, and it's your time to lead them boys out there and play how we all know you're capable of playing. No fear, no doubt, just go out there and play free and unafraid, and play like you did in high school again, play with some joy and enjoy the moment bro. I'm here for you every step of the way, you're gonna be one of the best PG's ever to come out of this university. Then we gonna finish it out together at the end of the year. It's your time bro

For Koenig, the exchange was freeing.

"That was such a compliment," said Koenig, who still had the text messages saved on his phone months later. "I respect Trae so much, for him to say that was a big boost for my confidence."

It also served as a passing of the torch. The Bronson Koenig era had officially begun in Madison.

Koenig caught the eye of college head coaches at a young age. Playing up a year on the AAU circuit, the fresh-faced preteen with a high-top fade sent recruiters scrambling for

Wisconsin's 2014 Final Four contest vs. Kentucky. Facing a team full of McDonald's All-Americans and fabled freshmen, Koenig was the best rookie on the floor for the first 20 minutes. With Jackson saddled with two fouls, Koenig played 16 of the 20 first-half minutes and responded with 11 points.

"Bronson was a man in that game," fellow classmate Nigel Hayes remarked. "In that game, against that team, he showed no fear. He was on the attack. That's big time."

"I had no doubts Bronson would be great," said Dekker. "I've known for a long time and probably had a better idea of what he could do than most. He's special."

The fact that Wisconsin lost that game to Kentucky and returned a senior backcourt in 2014-15 with Traevon Jackson and Josh Gasser delayed the Koenig coronation.

He began his sophomore season in an expanded role, but still coming off the bench in support. Koenig's numbers improved from his rookie campaign, but not by much, with him averaging 4.4 points and shooting 30 percent from 3-point range entering the Badgers' trip to Rutgers.

That's when everything changed on a twist of fate – or a twist of Jackson's foot.

Thrust into the starting role for UW's final 23 games of the season, Koenig flourished. After scoring in double figures just twice before Rutgers, he scored 10-plus points in eight of his first 10 games as the starting lead guard.

"I don't think we've ever had a backup as

well-prepared as Bronson," UW associate head coach Greg Gard said at the time. "Maybe this will be the spark that gets him going."

More like the kerosene.

While Koenig's minutes nearly doubled, his production nearly tripled.

Going from 19.8 per game to 35.0 minutes a night, Koenig jumped from 4.4 points per game to 11.5.

"He always had confidence, but I think we helped bring that out," Gasser explained. "We'd always tell him, 'You need to be

aggressive. You need to get the ball at the end of the shot clock.' He wanted to do the right thing for the team and be a good teammate to the older guys, so once he heard the coaches and his teammates tell him, 'You have the ball in your hands,' that's all he needed to hear. He took off from there."

"When I was coming off the bench I was guiding my shot more, because you never know when your next attempt will come and you want to make sure it goes in," Koenig revealed. "Once I became the starter and I wasn't looking over my shoulder any more I

basically just started to let it fly. I felt better. I never thought about it at all."

The results were dramatic.

Over the final 23 games of the season, Koenig shot 44.0 percent from outside the 3-point arc, hitting 48 of 109 attempts. All while maintaining a pristine assist-to-turnover ratio, dishing 2.5 dimes per turnover as a starter. In fact, Koenig coughed it up an average of just 1.3 times per 40 minutes over that stretch, the top mark of any major conference point guard in the country.

"Bronson surprised me a little bit," Gasser admitted. "I knew he could play, but to go from playing 15 minutes per game to playing all 40 minutes in some games and being productive the entire time was impressive."

"I wasn't surprised that he played so well," Ryan countered. "I will say though that anytime somebody who you know has talent reaches inside and uses it, it is a pleasant surprise. Everybody talks about Frank Kaminsky, and rightfully so, but it was Bronson Koenig's contributions and how well and steady he played that was the difference-maker this season."

As his freshman season foreshadowed, Koenig only got stronger once the calendar flipped to March. During the three-game Big Ten tournament, he shined with 16.3 points per game with a sparking 57 percent (9-for-17) shooting performance behind the arc. He played 116 of a possible 125 minutes, including 42 in the championship game win over Michigan State.

Nigel Hayes was fond of referring to Gasser as "Clutch Josh" during the season, but may have considered revising that to "Clutch Koenig" after the sophomore's late heroics against the Spartans.

Trailing by 11 with seven and a half minutes remaining, Koenig would score eight of UW's next 14 points including a go-ahead 3-pointer. But his best was yet to come. Down two in the waning moments, Koenig drove to the rim and drew a foul with 15 seconds remaining. With the poise of a hardened veteran, Koenig sunk a pair of free throws to tie the game and force overtime. For good measure, he would add another triple in the extra session and finish with 18 points, just one day after scoring a career-high 19 in a semifinal win over Purdue.

To the Badger that has known him the longest, Koenig's success came as no surprise.

"He has so much natural skill and physical gifts, but he's also worked really hard at it," Dekker gushed. "He has a knack for the big shot and a flair and poise that is uncommon. He gained a lot of confidence and exposure this year, but you're going to see an even better Bronson next year. I can't wait to see what he becomes.

"Big things are in store for him." ∎

Koenig started the final 24 games of the season and shot better than 40 percent from 3-point range on the season.
By Michael Conroy

UNTOUCHABLE

"It wasn't boredom at all, just ruthless efficiency."

"I've always been fond of the old saying that you measure a man by what it takes to discourage him," Bo Ryan would theorize after the 2015 season. "This team never got discouraged. After the Rutgers game, they came to practice the next day ready to work and what they did over the next six weeks proved that."

The next six weeks would prove that Wisconsin's loss at Rutgers was an anomaly. The next six weeks would validate the Badgers' lofty preseason ranking. The next six weeks would securely buckle UW into the driver's seat of the Big Ten race. The next six weeks would be historic.

Beginning with a 70-55 win over Nebraska on January 15, the Badgers would rip off 10 consecutive Big Ten wins, the team's longest conference winning streak since the 1941 national championship season.

But it wasn't just the night-in, night-out winning that was impressive. It was also UW's thorough dissection of opponents that had coaches like Northwestern's Chris Collins shaking their heads after a 40-minute fight with the Badgers.

"They're as good a team as we've played all year," Collins stated after a 65-50 defeat at the Kohl Center. "I say this all the time, when I'm not competing against them, I love watching them play. They're just a bunch of guys who are veterans – all juniors and seniors – who love playing with each other; they know each other inside and out. They play basketball the way it's supposed to be played."

Who could blame Collins for wanting to watch Wisconsin play? As *Sporting News* veteran writer Mike

A 70-55 win over Nebraska on Jan. 15 was the start of a 10-game winning streak for Nigel Hayes and the Badgers. *By David Stluka*

46

DeCourcy would later explain, "On the floor the beauty of the team was in how connected they were at both ends of the floor. They played a beautiful brand of basketball."

In the win over Nebraska that jumpstarted the Badgers' streak, Frank Kaminsky shook off his concussion and one-game absence to lead Wisconsin with 22 points. On his second shot of the game, a 3-pointer from the left wing, Kaminsky etched his name on the list of the school's elite by eclipsing the 1,000-point milestone. The senior standout would connect on 4 of 5 shots from 3-point range as the Badgers blistered the nets from deep and cruised to the win.

Perhaps the first indication that Wisconsin was clicking on all cylinders and would be just fine with sophomore Bronson Koenig at the point came five days later when a confident Iowa team visited the Kohl Center. The Hawkeyes came to Madison with a 4-1 record in the Big Ten and a spot in the AP Top 25. They would head back to Iowa City with a 32-point loss.

"Our home win over Iowa was an eye-opener because they came in on a roll and we stomped on them," Sam Dekker said of the 82-50 win over the rival Hawkeyes. "That doesn't happen in the Big Ten very often when good teams get rolled. That's pretty sweet when you can get a 30-point lead on teams you don't necessarily care for. It makes a statement."

Wisconsin played nearly flawlessly, jumping to an 18-point halftime cushion that would balloon to a 34-point lead in the second half. Koenig scored 13 points, but most impressively, the replacement point guard led a UW attack that had just one turnover on the night. And the one turnover was even debatable, as it came off a scorer's table correction of a shot-clock violation. The Badgers would score 82 points on a mere 53 possessions, for a Globetrotters-versus-Generals-esque 1.54 points per possession.

"The Iowa game stands out to me because we were so good that night and showed how good we can be. Iowa was a good team that was playing well at the time and they didn't like us," Josh Gasser added of a Hawkeyes team that had already posted road wins at North Carolina and Ohio State. "They didn't respect us or think we were that good. They really wanted to beat us, so to go out there and destroy them was pretty cool."

"That was big for us," Duje

Wisconsin tied a school record with just one turnover in its 82-50 dismantling of Iowa on Jan. 20.   *By Andy Manis*

Make 'Em Believe | 47

48

Dukan furthered. "It kind of sent a message and gave us confidence going into a tough stretch."

At 17-2 and ranked No. 6 in the country, Wisconsin would embark on a difficult two-game road swing that featured a visit to Ann Arbor, Michigan, and a rematch with a bitter Iowa team. This marked the second-straight year the Badgers would face that road double.

"One of the keys to the 2013-14 season was winning at Michigan and at Iowa back-to-back and I thought again this year, those two wins, going on the road, were really big," Ryan said. "You could see after the games from our guys' reactions that this wasn't just business as usual. They knew these were two teams that could beat anybody and we got both of them on the road."

The January 24 contest at Michigan provided a particular test for Wisconsin. Playing without leading scorer Caris Lavert (broken foot), the Wolverines would give an inspired effort for a boisterous Saturday-afternoon crowd.

For 39-and-a-half minutes, the Badgers played from ahead, leading by as many as 11 in the second half and still up four with 30 seconds left to play. But a pair of missed free throws opened the door for Michigan's late-game heroics. Leading 57-54 with 10 seconds remaining, the Badgers failed to execute a switch on a perimeter ball screen leaving Derrick Walton, Jr. open for a game-tying 3-pointer to send the game into overtime.

As Ryan huddled his team before the extra period he actually smiled, showing the poise of a 30-year veteran.

"OK, this will be good for us," Ryan

calmly told his team over the roar of "Hail to the Victors" blaring from the Michigan band. "What a great way to send a message by winning in overtime on the road, right? Let's get it done."

Wisconsin would seize control early in overtime, burning Michigan's 2-3 zone with a Kaminsky and-one and a Gasser triple from the wing.

"We didn't panic and I didn't go crazy in the huddle at the end of regulation," Ryan remembered of the 69-64 overtime win. "I said, 'We're here to take care of business and let's play the way we normally play and we'll be fine.'"

"If you want to pinpoint a resilient game for us, the win at Michigan would be a great example," Dukan said. "They really came to play, and we didn't close the game well at all in regulation but found a way to refocus in overtime. That was one of the first Big Ten games that we were tested. Big Ten setting, on the road, hostile environment, you need tests like that so later in the season when you face adversity, you know you can handle those situations."

The following weekend Wisconsin would have another opportunity to handle adversity, facing an Iowa team hungry for redemption.

"When we went down to Iowa for the rematch we were all prepared for them to bring their best effort," Gasser recalled. "Knowing they didn't really like us and having beaten them pretty badly just a week earlier, we figured it would be a different game."

The game played out differently than round one in Madison, but the result was the same as Wisconsin tallied an

Plagued by an ankle injury early in the season, Sam Dekker began to find his stride in January, including 15 points in the Badgers' overtime win at Michigan. *By Tony Ding*

imposing 74-63 win at Carver-Hawkeye Arena. When Iowa trimmed the Badgers' comfortable lead to five in the second half, Kaminsky and company vowed not to allow for a repeat of the collapse in Ann Arbor.

"The Michigan game was in our minds," Kaminsky said. "We weren't going to let that happen again."

Wisconsin didn't, pulling away by holding Iowa without a field goal for almost seven minutes. Kaminsky would lead the way with 24 points as the Badgers grabbed 15 offensive rebounds and scored 16 second-chance points.

"That was pretty satisfying," Gasser admitted. "I'd say one of our better wins."

Three days later, back in Madison, the Badgers would taste satisfaction again, this time in a rout of Big Ten heavyweight Indiana. Wisconsin would lead by as many as 32 before coasting to a 92-78 win, the team's 13th-straight home victory over the Hoosiers.

At one point of the winning streak, ESPN's Dan Dakich actually surmised during a broadcast that the Badgers might be so good that they were getting bored. In truth, it wasn't boredom at all, just ruthless efficiency.

"We were having fun and we developed a little swagger on the court that people may not have really known," Dekker hinted. "Not

"When we went to Iowa for the rematch we were all prepared for them to bring their best effort. That was pretty satisfying. I'd say it was one of our better wins." – Josh Gasser *By Icon Sportswire*

everybody on the team liked to talk, but some of us did. With our team it was never cocky or mean-spirited, but it was always to fire us up. We weren't going to be stupid about it but we liked to let people know that we're there."

For Dekker in particular, the Badgers' 10-game Big Ten win streak proved to be an awakening. Hampered by ankle and back injuries early in the season, the preseason All-Big Ten pick had yet to have a 20-point game and truly assert himself.

It took a little nudge from The Captain.

"I remember before our game at Nebraska, Sam hadn't practiced the night before because of a back injury," Gasser said. "During warm-ups I noticed him moving gingerly and kind of limping around. And I went up to him and said, 'Alright Sam, let's see how tough you are. Let's see what you're made of.' He looked back at me and I just walked away. I think he was almost offended and said to himself, 'OK, I'll show you how tough I am.' And he went out and played great, scoring 22 points with eight rebounds. That kind of stuff he took to heart. When he was challenged, he usually answered the bell."

"Yeah I remember Josh saying that," Dekker laughed before settling into a serious tone. "We all respect Josh so much, so when he kinda challenged me like that, I didn't want to let him down.

"There were three or four games this year that I didn't practice the night before and ended up playing really well. Even on the day of the Nebraska game, I didn't know if I was going to be able to play. But that game really felt good because it reminded me that I can still get going when not 100 percent and help our team. It was a pretty satisfying win."

Ryan also thought that win signified an important moment. Just over halfway through the Big Ten season, the Badgers had eyes on their goals.

"We had lost at Nebraska the year before, so if we were lacking any confidence, getting that one

---

The Badgers were sizzling hot by their Feb. 3 meeting with Indiana, and jumped out to a 32-point lead en route to their 13th-straight home win over the Hoosiers. *By David Stluka*

this year kind of gave us the idea that, 'Hey, we could win out.'"

Convincing wins over Illinois, Penn State and Minnesota pushed Wisconsin to 25-2 overall and 13-1 in the Big Ten. Astonishingly, the Badgers never trailed in the second half of any game during their 10-game win streak.

One win shy of clinching at least a share of the Big Ten championship, Gasser was asked of Dakich's comments about the Badgers looking bored.

"To get up for every game knowing that we're playing for a championship, that's fun," he said. "That's not boring at all." ∎

Sophomore Vitto Brown appeared in all but one game of the 2014-15 season and emerged as a valuable piece of Wisconsin's depth. *By David Stluka*

A FORGETTABLE TRIP

"You had to make light of the ridiculous situation."

From departure to return, the Badgers' February 24 trip to Maryland was forgettable.

Winners of 10 straight and owning a record of 13-1 in Big Ten play, the Badgers departed for College Park, Maryland just one win shy of clinching at least a share of the Big Ten championship. Even though Maryland, Michigan State and Purdue all sat a full three games behind in the standings with only four to play, Wisconsin knew it was about to face the most difficult stretch of its season.

UW's back-loaded conference slate featured a four-game finishing stretch that sandwiched a rivalry contest with Michigan State between three challenging road trips. The Badgers would visit the Terps, who were 22-5 and ranked 14th in the country at the time, then travel to Minnesota, where the Badgers had won just once in the last five trips, before wrapping up the regular season at 25th-ranked Ohio State, a team that featured one of the nation's top freshmen in guard D'Angelo Russell.

Wisconsin entered a perfect storm at Maryland's XFINITY Center. In their first season in the Big Ten the No. 14 Terrapins were looking to start new rivalries and school officials pointed to Wisconsin as a perfect challenger. The hosts were also looking to add a signature win to their resume, an

Frank Kaminsky's 18 points were not enough to overcome an 11-point halftime deficit at Maryland.
By Patrick Semansky

opportunity the fifth-ranked Badgers provided.

The capacity crowd and raucous student section was alive from the opening tip, helping Maryland to an 11-point (31-20) halftime lead. The Badgers' first-half struggles included 29.6 percent shooting, and

a 1-for-9 showing from 3-point range.

Wisconsin's vaunted front line of Nigel Hayes, Sam Dekker and Frank Kaminsky were a combined 6-for-17 in the first half as UW was held to a season-low 20 first-half points. Too often the Badgers settled for outside shots.

The halftime message was clear: feed the post.

The Badgers responded by scoring 12 of their first 15 points of the second half on the interior, with Kaminsky doing the heavy lifting with eight points in the paint in the opening six-and-a-half minutes.

Facing a second-half deficit for the first time in over six weeks, Ryan's squad foreshadowed a resolve that would become its signature late in the season. The Badgers would claw back to tie the game at 47-47 with 6:36 remaining on a Bronson Koenig 3-pointer.

"That second half is how we need to play all the time," Kaminsky noted afterward. "We can't wait for the game to come to us, we needed to be aggressive and utilize our strengths right from the start."

Despite the second-half resurgence, on this night, Maryland would not be denied. Dez Wells in particular would not be denied. The senior guard finished with 26 points, including a perfect 7-for-7 effort at the foul line. With the game knotted at 47-all, Wells scored the Terps' next six points to put Maryland in control. UW would trim the lead to three on two occasions in the final minutes but could never get the stop it needed.

As the final buzzer sounded on the Terrapins' 59-53 win, the PA announcer's plea to "Please do not rush the court" was no match for a frenzied student section that swallowed up Gary Williams Court in mere seconds.

Any doubts about Maryland fans embracing their new position in the Big Ten were quieted that evening. The loss would signal the end of Wisconsin's 10-game win streak, but Dekker could appreciate a great college basketball environment when he saw it.

"Man, this place is great," he said. "I can't say enough about how great their fans are. It was a pleasure to play here."

Disappointed but undeterred, Wisconsin would return home still just one game shy of a Big Ten championship.

"We were close a couple of times, but we just couldn't do it. It's definitely frustrating," UW's leading scorer, Kaminsky (18 points), said after the loss. "We've had a great season so far. We haven't really been tested like this many times. I think we're going to learn a lot from it."

Dez Wells' game-high 26 points were just the start of Wisconsin's troubles. *By Patrick Semansky*

Learn from it they did. Wisconsin wouldn't lose again until April.

The Badgers were so close to clinching the championship trophy on their trip to Maryland, they could almost touch it. Literally.

Completely unknown to Bo Ryan and his team, the Badgers' charter flight from Madison to Baltimore contained a little extra hardware. Among the team's baggage was the 2015 Big Ten championship trophy. An award that up until that point was not UW's property… yet.

Knowing a win over the Terrapins would result in at least a share of the Big Ten title, associate athletic director Justin Doherty was faced with the decision of whether or not to bring the championship trophy for a potential locker room celebration. The decision was simple – yes, in the event of a win, the Badgers would like to be able to recognize their accomplishment in the privacy of the visiting locker room. Knowing that Big Ten commissioner Jim Delany was coincidentally going to be in attendance, a plan for a subdued postgame presentation was put in place.

While the decision was simple, the execution of traveling with a 50-pound box without anyone on the team or staff knowing its contents was a whole lot trickier.

Where David Copperfield might pull off a "now-you-see-it, now-you-don't," Doherty, along with basketball staffers Katherine Vosters and Marc VandeWettering, executed a "you never saw it."

Internally, the covert plan was nicknamed "Operation Pineapple."

In a box marked "UW Development" the 2015 Big Ten championship trophy was snuck on and off the team charter under the guise of materials needed for entertaining UW donors in the Washington D.C. area. Seeing that the school's development office had never traveled with any materials in the past, explaining the contents of this mysterious box was more difficult.

Vosters and VandeWettering smuggled the trophy into the arena hidden within one of the team's oversized duffle bags.

"If anyone asked, it was a bag full of foam rollers," VandeWettering laughed. "Extremely heavy foam rollers."

Getting the "pineapple" into the arena wasn't the tricky part. Hiding it once it was unwrapped was the tall (heavy) task.

"We had the trophy tucked into the shower of the coaches' locker room," Vosters, UW's director of basketball operations explained. "The toughest part was getting it out of there after the game to a room where no one could see it.

"Weeks earlier, Coach Ryan had specifically said, 'I don't want to know anything about a trophy; when it is or where it is.' So Coach Ryan seeing the trophy, especially after a loss, was not an option. We also certainly didn't want Maryland to know we had it. That wouldn't have been good either."

Vosters and company had unpacked the trophy so it would be available for a celebration as soon as the team returned to the locker room. Given the game was still in doubt in the final minutes, there was no time to conceal the trophy and remove it before Ryan and his staff returned.

Wisconsin would go on to lose the game and as Ryan and his staff huddled in the coaches' locker room, Vosters couldn't help but keep a nervous eye on the concealing shower.

"After Coach exited the locker room to talk to the team, we started scrambling," Vosters added. "We had no idea how long we'd have until he returned so we had to get it out of there and to a different private location to repack it. The box was too heavy and big for one person to carry so we ended up sliding it down the hallway and into a family bathroom in another part of the arena where we could repack it and tape it shut. The whole thing was ridiculous."

Unfortunately for Vosters and the Badgers, that wouldn't even be the most ridiculous part of the road trip.

Following the game in College Park, Ryan was in a hurry to catch the team's charter flight home. He even explained that in the postgame press conference as Mark Turgeon graciously allowed Ryan to address the media after the Maryland coach had already begun his remarks.

This was probably one flight Ryan and his team wished they had missed.

Still sour from the loss, the Badgers boarded the aircraft just after 11 p.m. (ET) and settled in for a two-hour flight home to Madison. What is usually a hasty boarding and takeoff, this departure would not be as swift. First, the flight crew was unable to properly close the cabin door.

Ninety minutes later Vosters was scrambling for a Plan B.

"By this point, I was assuming we weren't going to get out," Vosters explained. "We had no bus – it was already 40 minutes away – or hotel or backup plane. We had started holding rooms at a bunch of hotels around the Baltimore airport area when a mechanic showed up. He eventually got the door secured with some magic spray or something. In fact, I remember Coach Ryan

saying to me, 'Kat, make sure we pack that spray on our next trip.' I think he was joking, but I wasn't sure," Vosters laughed.

Perhaps the door not closing should have been an omen.

Now after midnight and about 45 minutes into the quiet redeye, a whispered rumor began to spread throughout the sleepy cabin.

"One of the plane's engines is not functioning properly and we will be making an emergency landing in Pittsburgh."

Instant perspective.

Many of the 41-person travel party were tipped off that something was amiss when the plane began to descend far too early, and rapidly, into the anticipated two-hour flight.

With the pilot later describing the cockpit as "too hectic to make an announcement" the team was left with a flight attendant as the intermediary. Showing no signs of panic or urgency, the flight attendant remained professional and calm.

"We're not trying to scare you," she would explain.

Too late.

"The captain doesn't like the way one of the engines is performing, so we want to get this airplane on the ground as soon as possible."

For those still awake, thoughts of Wisconsin's slow start against Maryland and second-half comeback for naught began to disappear. Ten minutes after being notified of the issue, the team's Embraer ERJ-145 was landing on a runway filled with ambulances, fire trucks and emergency personnel. Unsettling to say the least.

Once everyone was assured that there was no imminent danger, a difficult question surfaced.

What do you do with a 41-person travel party at 1 a.m. in Pittsburgh when you have no hotel, transportation or plan for the next day?

Quite a challenge for Vosters, who was in

her first year coordinating Wisconsin's logistics.

"When we were delayed getting out because of the door, I remember somebody remarking that this is a director of operations worst nightmare," Vosters said. "They were wrong. Landing in a new city at 1 a.m. with absolutely nothing planned… that is a worst nightmare."

Within a minute of landing, Vosters and program assistant Marc VandeWettering were working their way down a list of a dozen hotels near Pittsburgh International Airport. Most of the hotels had no vacancies due to bad weather in the area cancelling a number of flights, but Vosters was able to book a total of 24 rooms spread across three hotels.

Despite the predicament, Ryan played the role of comic relief.

"I picked a bad day to stop sniffing glue," Ryan deadpanned a line from the famous movie *Airplane*.

By the time the team stuffed into seven different utility vans and settled into their respective hotels, the clock was past 2 a.m.

"We probably shouldn't even say this, but we had people riding on top of luggage, in the backs of trucks, on each other's laps. By that point, everybody was just like, 'Get me to bed,'" said Vosters.

Surely the next day had to go smoother.

Not so fast.

Just as Vosters believed she had secured a new charter plane and bus to pick everyone up, that plane was delayed in South Carolina and the bus broke down outside one of the hotels.

Unbelievable.

"It might sound strange, but one of my favorite off-court memories from the season is actually when our plane had to make the emergency landing on the Maryland trip," Dekker recalled of the team hanging out in the impromptu hotel and organizing paper football tournaments. "We were all salty after

the loss and that unexpected detour and hassle of staying overnight in Pittsburgh helped us get over the loss. You had to make light of the ridiculous situation, and that extra time hanging with each other was valuable."

The Badgers would finally land safely in Madison a little before 2 p.m. (CT) the next day. A date with Michigan State and the Big Ten championship trophy was just four days away. ■

BIG TEN CHAMPS

"What do you do with Frank Kaminsky?"

For Wisconsin, March 1, 2015 was the perfect storm. Still smarting from a loss at Maryland five days prior, the Badgers were one win away from clinching a Big Ten championship. The only thing that stood in the way of reaching a goal they had talked about since the summer was No. 25 Michigan State, perhaps the team's most storied rival in the Big Ten.

If that wasn't enough motivation, it was also Senior Day. March 1 would mark the final game at the Kohl Center for one of the most adored senior classes in school history, Frank Kaminsky, Josh Gasser, Traevon Jackson and Duje Dukan. And while it wasn't known at the time, it would also serve as the Madison swan song for beloved junior Sam Dekker.

Typically, Senior Day is a well of emotions and often produces tears as the players are introduced pregame, walking out arm-in-arm with their parents. There was a different feel on this occasion.

"Senior Day was emotional in the sense that it was our last time playing in the Kohl Center and in front of the home fans," Dukan explained. "But there weren't many tears or anything from the seniors because we all knew what that game meant and how much of the season was left in front of us. It was more of determination and anxiousness."

The seniors, and Kaminsky in particular, would not waste the opportunity.

Television analyst Dan Bonner opened the CBS broadcast saying, "The big problem for anybody guarding Wisconsin is, what do you do with Frank Kaminsky?"

Michigan State would have no answer. Kaminsky dazzled with a season-high 31 points, hitting 11 of 17 shots from the field including 3-for-4 from beyond the 3-point arc. After the game, Spartans coach Tom Izzo was left with little else to do but pay his respects.

Michigan State had no answer for Frank Kaminsky, who had a season-high 31 points, 8 rebounds, 3 assists, 3 blocks and 2 steals. *By John Fisher | Cal Sport Media*

Nigel Hayes and the Badgers jumped to a big lead after shooting nearly 60 percent from the field in the first half vs. the Spartans. *By John Fisher | Cal Sport Media*

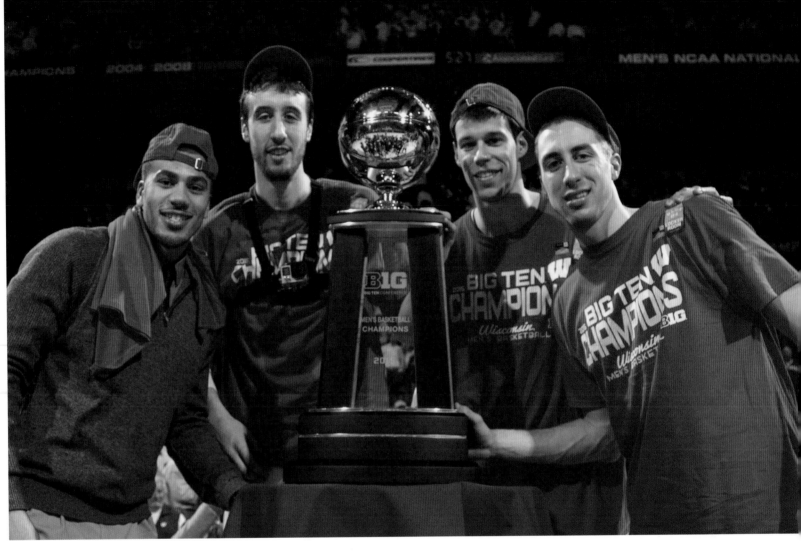

"I thought the kid was sensational," Izzo said of Kaminsky. "He just kept making big shot after big shot, whether it be a 3 or on the floor. He's the most versatile kid that our league has seen in a long, long time."

"My job was easy today, get the ball to Frank and get out of the way," Gasser, who had nine points, would laugh in the locker room after the game. "I honestly found myself just watching him at times, he was that good."

Wisconsin seized control early and opened up an 11-point halftime lead, dominating the points in the paint by a margin of 24 to 6.

"Against Maryland, we settled for a lot of shots and we didn't want that to happen again," Kaminsky remembered from the game before. "The second half of the Maryland game, we got the ball inside and some good things happened for us. We just tried to get that going from the start of the game (vs. Michigan State). It helped to push a lead out and never look back."

The Badgers' lead would later rise to 22 points on a jumper from Nigel Hayes, who scored 14 points. MSU closed to within 11 with 2:28 remaining, but Kaminsky slammed the door with a ridiculous baseline floater off the glass and an emphatic block at the other end. The sellout crowd rose to its feet with the serenading chant of "Frank The Tank! Frank The Tank!" coming from the Grateful Red student section filling the arena.

As the final seconds ticked off the clock, Gasser dribbled the ball out, pumping his fists and bathing in the standing ovation raining down on the court. The Badgers had just clinched the 18th Big Ten championship in school history and the fourth under Bo Ryan.

"I had this day circled from the moment the schedule came out," Gasser said from under a red championship hat. "Win the Big Ten championship, at home, on Senior Day, have to play your tail off against a good team, a rival, in front of a great crowd... what more could you want? It's a perfect script."

Kaminsky's performance left Michigan State coach Tom Izzo saying, "I've never been so impressed with a player in our league since maybe 'Big Dog' (Purdue's Glenn Robinson) back in the day." *By David Stluka*

your final game at home and winning the Big Ten championship was surreal," Kaminsky remembered after the season, still wearing the Cheshire grin. "We had wanted to do something special that season and living that moment was unbelievable."

"Senior Day was, without a doubt, one of the most fun nights of my career," Gasser echoed.

"This was a special senior class," Ryan offered. "With all they accomplished, how they got better, how they gave for each other, they'll be remembered for a long time. I got a little misty during the pregame ceremony watching those young men walk out with their families and thinking back on their careers. I was extremely proud that day."

To a man, the Badgers would leave the Kohl Center that day elated, but reciting the same refrain.

"This is satisfying and we'll celebrate, but we still want a whole lot more out of this season," Kaminsky voiced for his teammates.

On a curved, sweeping wall of the Badgers locker room hang a series of photos and captions that commemorate the greatest moments in Kohl Center history. They will no doubt be adding March 1, 2015. ∎

The postgame scene was pandemonium. The Badgers took a victory lap, running through the stands high-fiving the student section. Kaminsky banged on the drums of the pep band and Hayes sidled up to Ryan and simply said, "Pops, you're going up," before he and his teammates lifted their head coach into the air for a curtain call.

Atop a hastily assembled on-court stage, the four seniors, including Jackson, who was still nursing a broken foot and watched the game in street clothes from the bench, hoisted the Big Ten championship trophy into the air. Kaminsky took the microphone and addressed the crowd.

"This team is like a family to me," he remarked as enraptured fans responded with an "awwwww" sound. "They treat me terrible sometimes. But that's just how family is. I'm just so happy."

One by one the Badgers climbed atop a ladder to cut a ceremonial piece of net, Kaminsky's GoPro capturing every second. He had received it as a Christmas gift, and the sight of the miniature camera strapped to Kaminsky's chest would become a championship ritual as the season unfolded.

"Riding that emotional high of playing

FRANK THE TANK

"Awesome is the perfect word to describe Kaminsky's career."

As Josh Gasser and Ben Brust walked off the Kohl Center floor on November 19, 2013, they exchanged a laugh over the improbable feat, the certain-to-be obscure trivia answer, they had just witnessed.

"In 20 years, no one is going be able to guess who holds the Wisconsin record for most points in a game," Brust chuckled.

"They're going to say, 'Frank who? Frank Kaminsky? Are you kidding me?' No one will ever know that," Gasser agreed.

Gasser might be right. People may not remember that Frank Kaminsky scored 43 points against North Dakota to set the school's single-game record. They may not remember it because after all Kaminsky accomplished, the 43-point performance turned into a mere footnote on what became the most celebrated career in Wisconsin history.

It was also one of the most improbable careers.

A few days before heading to the 2015 Big Ten Tournament in Chicago, Frank Kaminsky crammed his larger-than-life, 7-foot frame into a Kohl Center studio, hardly bigger than a phone booth. On an off-day for the team, here was Kaminsky accepting Big Ten Player of the Year honors during an interview on Big Ten Network.

BTN studio host Mike Hall began by asking the simple question, "Your freshman year you averaged 1.8 points per game. If I had told you back then that, as a senior, you'd be the Big Ten Player of the Year, what would 19-year old Frank have said to me?"

"I would have called you a liar," Kaminsky deadpanned. "I couldn't have expected this with the progression I made

By John Fisher | Cal Sport Media

"When Frank got to campus he was goofy and I didn't think he could play right away. But to his credit, he knew he had it in him somewhere and he kept working." – Josh Gasser
By Icon Sportswire

throughout my career. It's been awesome."

Awesome is the perfect word to describe Kaminsky's career.

As a gangly prep at Benet Academy 25 miles west of downtown Chicago, Kaminsky had high-major height and skills, but didn't have the big-time scholarship offers to match. Despite an athletic family tree that features a 6-foot-10 father, also named Frank, who played collegiate basketball at Lewis University and a mother, Mary, who stands 6 feet tall and played volleyball at Northwestern, "Little Frankie," as he is

known at home, was only recruited by mid-level Illinois schools and Northwestern and DePaul.

When Wisconsin offered the 6-foot-11 big man who at that point was admittedly gun-shy of going in the paint, Kaminsky nearly committed on the spot. The decision to attend school in Madison was easy. Seeing time on the court was not.

"When Frank got to campus I don't know what I thought of him," Gasser confessed. "He was goofy and I didn't think he could play right away. He really wanted to play, but

he wasn't good enough. But to his credit, he knew he had it in him somewhere and he kept working."

"We knew Frank had skills and potential when he got to campus, but in the first couple years, he hadn't shown us that he was ready to play," Bo Ryan added. "He had some growing to do, plus there was a pretty good big man in front of him. A guy that when it was all said and done, taught Frank a lot."

That big man ahead of him on the depth chart was 6-foot-10 Jared Berggren, who was two years older than Kaminsky. Biding his time, Kaminsky averaged fewer than three points and two rebounds per game in his first two seasons at Wisconsin.

"As a freshman and sophomore, he wasn't even on our scouting report," Penn State head coach Patrick Chambers said of Kaminsky.

Finally given the chance to start in 2013-14, Kaminsky didn't waste the opportunity. The now 7-footer turned himself into a matchup nightmare. With an almost unfair combination of nimble footwork in the post and a feathery touch from 3-point range, Kaminsky jumped to 13.9 points and 6.4 rebounds per game as a junior. His complete arsenal was on display in a 28-point, 11-rebound Elite Eight masterpiece against Arizona that sent the Badgers to the 2014 Final Four and launched Kaminsky into the national spotlight.

That brings us to April 25, 2014.

On the heels of a standout NCAA tournament showing, the 21-year old junior had put himself squarely in the crosshairs of NBA draft personnel. Kaminsky's father was hearing from agents and professional executives at a rate with which he could hardly keep up. After seeking consultation and leaning on Ryan to solicit feedback from pro scouts, Kaminsky decided to return to Wisconsin for his senior season. The reasons were many and the Badgers big man took to his personal blog to explain them.

I made a commitment to the University of Wisconsin, and they made a commitment to me. Who would have thought that I would be in this position at the end of last season? If any, they wouldn't have been willing to bet on that. If you know anything about me, you would know that I pride myself on being loyal. I will always be loyal to anyone or anything that I care about, and I care about this school and this basketball team. They have become part of my identity and who I am.

I love this place. I am exactly where I need to be. The University of Wisconsin has provided me with an opportunity to be the best I can be. So why not provide the University of Wisconsin with the best basketball team that has stepped foot on this campus?

"This year, this run... it started with Frank saying he was coming back," Ryan would divulge after the season. "Whatever he decided on, we were going to go with and support him. But everybody was happy that he wanted to be a big part of what was coming."

An afterthought his first two years on campus, Kaminsky became a household name as a junior and a star as a senior. *By David Stluka*

The son of collegiate standouts "Big Frank" and Mary Kaminsky, "Little Frankie" always had the genes to be great.
By John Fisher | Cal Sport Media

It's true that Kaminsky returned to Madison because he loved college. But he also returned to get better. The summer of 2014 would not serve as a victory lap.

"Frank started to see the importance in taking care of all the small details that, before, he may have thought were insignificant," strength and conditioning coach Erik Helland observed. "Things like diet, sleep, things he was doing for recovery, the quality of his work in the weight room, organizing his time better, being prepared to

do your job when you enter that environment. He asked himself the question, 'What kind of an effort and quality do we bring to this?' Good enough doesn't work. If you want to achieve extraordinary things, you can't bring ordinary effort to the table."

"I worked really hard behind the scenes in the summer before my senior year," Kaminsky confirmed. "I knew we had a really good team coming back and I wanted to make this one of the greatest seasons in college basketball history for our team."

Kaminsky's meteoric rise also meant the burden of expectation. Tabbed as a preseason All-American, *Sports Illustrated* plastered his photo on its season preview issue and ESPN.com went so far as to rank him the No. 1 player in college basketball entering the year. For a player who was even overshadowed on his high school team (by teammate David Sobolewski, who would play at Northwestern), Kaminsky wasn't comfortable with the spotlight.

"This was honestly my thought process: I didn't want all that attention going into my senior year. Things like being ranked the number one player in the country and all of that. I didn't want that pressure put on me and I just wanted to go out and play.

"I'm the type of guy who thinks through situations with both positive outcomes and negative outcomes and I felt the media was almost a negative thing because they were building me up to be this certain player and if I didn't fulfill that it would have been embarrassing."

To that end, when Kaminsky was notified he was the Big Ten Preseason Player of the Year, his candid response was, "No, why? I don't want to be. Why would they pick me?"

He knew the answer to his own question, and deep down, he knew his preseason hype was undeniable.

"I hated the media attention at the start," Kaminsky conceded. "For two years at Wisconsin I was a nobody and didn't have to talk to anyone. Then all of a sudden everything was different. It was kind of a shock to the system and I didn't know how to handle it. But once the season got rolling and things started to go my way, I got more comfortable with the attention.

"The line I used was, 'I still hate doing interviews, I just hate it a little less,'" Kaminsky joked.

Kaminsky also got comfortable with the media attention because he started to have fun with it. Perhaps his greatest trait was that, through it all, he never took himself seriously. He began to reveal the "Frankie" that those close to him have seen for years.

"Frankie's always been a really fun-loving kid who likes to make people laugh," his mother Mary said with a smile. "I was glad to see him not taking himself too seriously, because the pressure could get to you."

"When Frankie was younger and he started to grow so quickly, he was so much taller than everybody and he was looking for a way to fit in," revealed his father, Frank. "I think the goofiness and the silliness was his mechanism to fit in with everybody at that time."

That silliness would manifest itself over and over again during the season, charming media and fans along the way.

Take the *ESPN The Magazine* photo shoot of Kaminsky in the Animal House-inspired "COLLEGE" sweater, or the images of him riding his scooter with Bucky Badger on the back holding on for dear life. On the court after the Big Ten tournament championship, there was Kaminsky strapped with his GoPro camera across his chest, lunging to catch the falling confetti on his tongue. When ESPN's College GameDay asked him to play along with a bit where announcers held a fantasy draft of college players, Kaminsky filmed a reaction to his mock selection by feigning passing out. On another outtake, he collapsed into his hands pretending to sob.

"I'm one of the goofiest people I know," Kaminsky readily admits. "There aren't many things that I do very seriously. I just like having fun in a lot of different situations."

He also got very comfortable in his own skin. For proof, look no further than the viral dance-off video set to Taylor Swift's "Shake It Off."

"Early in the season I got a message on Facebook from an on-campus a Capella group called Fundamentally Sound asking if I would help them do a music video," Kaminsky explained. "I was like, 'Sure, no problem.' Then I get there and they tell me they're going to have me do a dance-off. I said, 'Hold on a minute.'"

Evidently he didn't need much arm-twisting. The result was an utterly ridiculous sequence of flailing arms and hip-swiveled dance moves that have been viewed over a quarter million times on YouTube. His teammates just shook their heads at the antics of their self-deprecating big man with the dry wit.

"I think it even starts with how he looks. He's a different-looking guy," Sam Dekker smirked. "He's 7 feet tall and he's got that sleepy look about him. But he lights up the room with weird comments and doesn't care what people think."

"He was definitely immature when he started here," Gasser added. "And even as a senior he was immature, but this time it was in a good way. He was still goofy and could have fun, but he could flip the switch and lock in when it was time to focus and play basketball."

"He's Napoleon Dynamite at times; I'm sure he's a lot of different characters I don't even know," Ryan remarked. "But the one thing I do know is he's a heck of a player."

What would unfold over the next six months was the stuff of legend.

By David Stluka

▲A self-proclaimed "goofball," Kaminsky never missed an opportunity to see humor in a situation like riding a shuttle at the Final Four or a routine photoshoot. *By Charlie Neibergall*
▶*Courtesy of UW Athletics*

Kaminsky began the season as just the third preseason Associated Press All-American in school history and, somehow, still exceeded expectations. Producing one dominating performance after another, Kaminsky positioned himself on the short list for national player of the year by Christmas. Among the Big Ten's leaders in nearly every statistical category, no player had more value to his team. That was verified in early January when the Badgers dropped the one game Kaminsky missed with a concussion, a head-scratching 67-62 loss against a Rutgers team that finished 2-16 in the Big Ten.

With Kaminsky on the floor, the Badgers outscored opponents by a staggering 577 points. Without Kaminsky, Wisconsin was actually outscored by four.

The versatile player that sports radio personality Dan Patrick once quipped could be nicknamed "The Spork," Kaminsky spent much of the season as the only player in the country leading his team in points, rebounds, assists, blocks and steals.

"Frank is interesting because he is one of the least arrogant people you'll meet, but he had this matter-of-fact attitude and approach that no other big man in college basketball was as good as him," Gasser said. "That

sounds cocky, but it really wasn't. It was almost just a realization of his self-worth.

"On the court he wouldn't talk trash or act too cool. He would just go out there and beat you."

"We knew Frank had a chance to be good, but I don't think anybody saw him as the national player of the year," Dekker acknowledged. "His confidence was so ridiculously high his senior year and his skill set was impossible to defend. He was our best player every night and, no question, the key to our success. He handled all the attention so well and never changed. When your best player is that consistent and selfless, that raises up everyone."

To support Dekker's claim, when asked which of his team-leading stats he was most proud of, Kaminsky responded, "The assists column. I didn't expect that one, but I think I'm a good teammate and take pride in that. I've said it many times, and it's the honest truth, I'd be just as happy scoring two points per game as long as we're winning."

"What Frank achieved is an amazing accomplishment," Helland gushed. "The fact that he is able to achieve such a high level of personal success, and do so to the benefit of his entire team, is an amazing thing. And truly, that's what separates the greatest players in our game, what kind of effect they have on a group. Frank made everyone better."

"Frank was an inspiration to the other guys with how hard he worked and how he improved," Ryan added. "That sends a message to the younger players on the team. They see that it doesn't happen by accident and that there is a lot of work involved. But it also gives everyone hope."

As the player of the year race narrowed to Kaminsky and Duke's freshman phenom Jahlil Okafor, Kaminsky seemed to find another level. He would leave no doubt who was the nation's best.

In his final curtain call at the Kohl Center, on Senior Day against Michigan State, Kaminsky was simply unstoppable. With the Big Ten championship on the line, Kaminsky scored 31 points in seemingly every way possible and willed Wisconsin to its first of three championships in March. The performance earned the unbridled adoration of Michigan State's Tom Izzo, who had a front row seat from the visitor's bench.

"I've never been so impressed with a

player in our league since maybe 'Big Dog' (Purdue's Glenn Robinson) back in the day," Izzo said breathlessly. "I thought the kid was sensational. He just kept making big shot after big shot, whether it be a 3 or on the floor. He's the most versatile kid that our league has seen in a long, long time. I would like to give my early vote that Kaminsky is, no question, the best player in the country this year."

The sentiment would become unanimous. Four days after Kaminsky's overwhelming of Michigan State, ESPN.com's Wooden Watch, which had been handicapping the player of the year race all season would say:

His season averages – 18.8 points, 8.3 rebounds per game – only hint at his brilliance. If the consensus hadn't been formed already, Sunday hardened it like concrete. Officially, the Wooden Award race will continue through the next couple of weeks. Really, it's already over. Kaminsky will win. Even better? He deserves to.

On March 23, *Sports Illustrated* named Kaminsky its Player of the Year, presenting the scruffy superstar on its cover – his third such appearance in a 12-month span. The image featured Kaminsky, clad in his red Wisconsin jersey and shorts standing in front of a 1978-built M60A3 Main Battle Tank. Playing off his "Frank the Tank" nickname, the photo shoot came together just outside

Kaminsky's whirlwind media blitz included a *Sports Illustrated* photoshoot in 25-degree weather in front of a retired army tank. *By Patrick Herb*

Madison at American Legion Post 360 in Waunakee. However, conditions weren't ideal.

"That was one of the crazier media things we did. We had snow and freezing rain the night before so the photographer had to clear off the tank and dig out a place for me to stand. Plus, it was like 25 degrees, so being out there in shorts and a jersey was freezing," Kaminsky described.

"I remember standing out there for a few pictures, then jumping into a running car with the heat blasting to warm up. Then going back out to shoot a few more and then get back in the car, repeating that for a half hour. It was fun, though, and the cover turned out pretty cool."

That was only the beginning of Kaminsky's cool final weeks of the season. He would interview comedian Will Ferrell as a correspondent for Access Hollywood, fly on a

"I hated the media attention at the start, but once things started to go my way, I got more comfortable with the attention." – Frank Kaminsky *By David Stluka*

Kaminsky swept every National Player of the Year award, including the Oscar Robertson Trophy and AP Player of the Year awards. *By Kiichiro Sato*

By Charlie Neibergall

private plane to star in the first-ever ESPN College Basketball Awards Show, take his mother to the White House Correspondents' Dinner and sweep every national player of the year award. Kaminsky became the first Wisconsin player to take home the Naismith Award, the Wooden Award, the Oscar Roberson Trophy and the AP Player of the Year honor.

"It was all very humbling," an appreciative Kaminsky said. "I've never been about individual accolades and I just kept thanking my teammates, coaches, family and everyone who helped me on this crazy ride."

When his transcendent collegiate career finally ended in the national championship in Indianapolis, it was Badger Nation that was thanking him. A true student-athlete who earned his degree that May, Kaminsky's rags-to-riches basketball story left fans of college athletics feeling indebted.

"I think Frank is what college basketball is about," Gasser admired. "All too often, when guys don't play as a freshman or sophomore they either transfer or just give up and not work hard. He didn't do either of those. In fact, he worked harder."

"I've never seen a story quite like his," a grateful Ryan added. "You can ask anybody in the country and they'll say the same thing. You just don't go from where he was to the best player in the country. Frank really didn't pout about not playing. He would work hard in practice and he just kept developing. Those are the kind of stories that come along once every great while. That's what makes them special, because they're so rare." ∎

OHIO STATE-MENT

"This was a one-game championship, a chance to make a statement."

The Badgers celebrated a share of the Big Ten regular season championship in front of a raucous Kohl Center crowd with a win over Michigan State. They would quietly celebrate the outright conference crown a few days later in the cramped visiting locker at Minnesota's Williams Arena after a convincing 76-63 win over the Gophers.

"Winning a share of the title against Michigan State and then winning it outright on a rival's court like Minnesota is pretty sweet," Frank Kaminsky said after scoring a game-high 25 points.

"We had a ton of Wisconsin fans in the building and we could hear them, especially the Grateful Red section way up in the upper deck," added Sam Dekker, who scored 20 on the night. "Between the fans and the Big Ten championship on the line, we had a lot of motivation."

On the surface, it seemed Dekker and company would have far less motivation in their final regular season contest. With the league championship and the number one seed for the Big Ten tournament already secured, the Badgers traveled to 23rd-ranked Ohio State with little other than NCAA tournament seeding at stake.

"In the last game at Ohio State, we had already kind of celebrated the Big Ten championship twice and so I was a little concerned that we weren't going to bring it," Josh Gasser admitted. "We had gone to Ohio State and gotten beat badly before, and that thought crossed my mind."

"We knew we were going on the road against a really good team, but I wasn't worried about a let-down," Bo Ryan explained. "After already clinching the Big Ten championship, we kind of treated this as the first game of the postseason. I told the guys before the game that this was a one-game championship. It was a chance to make a statement."

While Wisconsin was tracking a number one seed in the Big Dance, Ohio State was looking to bolster a résumé that could use a signature win. Instead, it was the Badgers who put a giant exclamation point on

Josh Gasser got the best of Ohio State All-American D'Angelo Russell, who said, "He did a great job, as you can see by my stats. He's a tough defender, and a great defender."
By Jay LaPrete

74

Duje Dukan and the Badgers handed the Buckeyes their second-worst loss in 17 years at Value City Arena. *By Icon Sportswire*

one of the greatest regular seasons in school history.

Wisconsin rolled to a 72-48 win, handing Ohio State its second-worst loss in 17 years at Value City Arena and spoiling Senior Day for four Buckeyes upperclassmen. The win pushed the Badgers' record to 28-3 overall and 16-2 in the Big Ten, equaling the school-record for conference wins.

Any doubts about Wisconsin – as well an OSU crowd of over 18,000 – were quieted in dominating fashion.

"I wasn't surprised we played well at Ohio State," Dekker relayed. "We had no pressure on us. They were fighting for seeding and we could just play freely. It ended up being one of those nights where almost anything worked. When we were rolling like that it was so much fun. Everybody clicked, the starters, the bench."

Seven different Badgers scored in the first nine minutes of the game and by the time Duje Dukan splashed a 3-pointer from the wing, UW was off and running with a 23-9 lead. The cushion would swell to 17 points before the Buckeyes made one final push. Ohio State used a 9-0 run to pull within 46-39 with 13 minutes remaining and incite the team's largest crowd of the season.

"When we cut it to seven, I said, 'All right, we're back. We got our team back. Here we are. This is my team,'" Ohio State coach Thad Matta said after the game. "But they sort of took it to another level with the execution."

Wisconsin scored the next 16 points, sending Ohio State fans to the exits with over six minutes still remaining. That level of execution was nothing new to a Badgers team that had gotten remarkably good at silencing opposing arenas.

"Moments like that made you realize how good we were. We could be scary," Dekker boasted. "We proved our point that we could walk into a tough place against a good team and match that intensity. I had a losing record vs. OSU and wanted to finish with a win. We hadn't won there too often and had suffered some bad losses in that building. It felt nice to turn the tables and give them one."

For Ohio native Nigel Hayes, the runaway victory in Columbus was particularly sweet. *By Jay LaPrete*

Over the two-year stretch, the Badgers were an incredible 18-5 on the road and 19-3 in neutral venues, posting the most wins and highest win percentage away from home of any major conference team in the country.

"We had a lot of road success over the last two years largely because we were an older team that had the right kind of voices in the locker room," Ryan theorized. "We had a team that was willing to share the ball and guys had the ability to score but weren't worried about their own numbers outside of the offense. We had guys that will be playing at the next level, but they weren't playing for the next level."

Another point Wisconsin's deconstruction of Ohio State served was to confirm Gasser's position as one of the conference's, and perhaps the nation's, top defenders. The next day the fifth-year senior was named to the Big Ten's All-Defensive Team for a school-record third time and his efforts on the final two Sundays of the conference season were a snapshot of why.

In Columbus, Gasser drew the challenging assignment of shadowing the Buckeyes' soon-to-be lottery pick, D'Angelo Russell. The freshman guard was among the Big Ten's leading scorers and had just posted 28 points in each of his last two outings. Russell

Wisconsin's win at Ohio State finished off a 16-2 Big Ten season, which equaled the best mark in school history. *By Jay LaPrete*

finished with 17 points (many of which came against other UW defenders), but Gasser frustrated him into 1-for-7 shooting from 3-point range and five turnovers.

"He did a great job, as you can see by my stats. He's a tough defender, and a great defender," Russell allowed.

When Ryan was asked if Gasser made Russell work hard, he replied, "I think Josh makes a lot of people work."

Michigan State's leading scorer, Travis Trice, would concur the following weekend. In the Big Ten tournament championship game, Gasser hounded Trice into one of his worst games of the season with just six points on 2-for-8 shooting and 0-for-4 from 3-point range.

"He didn't win the award, but to me, Josh was the best defensive player in the Big Ten," Kaminsky said. "That game against Russell and Ohio State... there aren't many guys that can frustrate an All-American like that."

Always humble and understated, Gasser was reluctant to take credit.

"We found a way to do a good job on D'Angelo Russell and on their whole team. We really handled them," Gasser said. "It was one of those games where we maybe didn't have the same laser focus we did for other games and we were still able to go on the road and win by 20. That was a sign that we might be pretty good."

Pretty good? Yeah, always understated. ∎

Make 'Em Believe | 77

BIG TEN CHAMPS, AGAIN

"Our goal all along was to be considered the best team ever at Wisconsin."

"I don't like to share."

Frank Kaminsky let his feelings be known in the United Center locker room moments before the Badgers took the floor for the Big Ten tournament championship game.

"If we're Big Ten champs, then we're Big Ten champs alone."

Kaminsky's teammates felt the same way.

"When we got to Chicago, we had obviously already clinched the Big Ten regular season but that wasn't enough," Josh Gasser explained after the season. "We really wanted to be the class of the Big Ten, and in order to do that, you have to win both championships. So we took that tournament seriously."

Wisconsin had sprinted to a record of 28-3, the best start in school history. The Badgers were just the third Big Ten team in the last 20 years to post 28 regular-season wins, and the team's 16-2 conference record equaled the best mark in program history. But they were greedy.

"Our goal all along was to be considered the best team ever at Wisconsin," Sam Dekker said. "And that wasn't an arrogant thing in the least, we just felt like we had the type of team to make history. But we also knew that the postseason was where we would be defined."

If you were defining the Badgers after their three-day run in Chicago, you'd start with words like resiliency, guile, toughness and end with words like winners.

The script Wisconsin had followed during the regular season would be rewritten in Chicago. Only twice in 16 Big Ten regular season wins had the Badgers trailed in the second half. They would face second-half deficits in all three games of the Big Ten tournament.

"I think we learned a little something

Bronson Koenig averaged 16.3 points per game at the 2015 Big Ten Tournament. *By Robert Campbell*

about ourselves during the Big Ten tournament," Kaminsky would say later. "We had to dig deep and battle in all three games. We faced adversity and came out on top. That could only help us moving forward."

By the time the Badgers boarded their bus to Chicago on Thursday evening, the Big Ten tournament was already four games old and a fifth was underway. As the tournament's No. 1 seed, the Badgers enjoyed a bye into Friday's quarterfinals where Michigan was waiting. The Wolverines used an impressive 73-55 win over Illinois on Thursday afternoon to advance to the rematch with the Badgers.

Six weeks earlier Wisconsin had escaped Ann Arbor with an overtime win over a Wolverines team that was now playing for its postseason life. As Michigan coach John Beilein noted before the game, "We have nothing to lose."

For 35 minutes, the Wolverines played that way. Michigan led by as many as nine in the first half and tied the game at 54-54 with about six minutes remaining on a 3-point jumper from sophomore Zak Irvin. But much as Wisconsin did in the overtime session on January 24 at Crisler Arena, the Badgers put the clamps on Michigan down the stretch. A decisive 9-2 UW run featured a pair of interior buckets from Kaminsky, but the play that would symbolize the Badgers' Big Ten tournament came moments later.

Kaminsky said after the game that energy made the difference over the final minutes, and he might as well have been describing himself.

Protecting a 58-56 lead with just under four minutes left, Kaminsky was unable to finish a post move from the low block. But he wouldn't be denied. Kaminsky out-wrestled Michigan forward Kameron Chatman for the loose ball rebound, diving to the floor to gain possession before shoveling it to Gasser. Two passes later, Dekker knocked down three of his team-high 17 points and put the Badgers in control.

Instead of an embarrassing early exit that would have all but extinguished any chances of a No. 1 seed in the NCAA tournament, Wisconsin was exhaling on its way to the semifinals against Purdue.

"We hadn't played from behind much in games but really had to fight all three games in Chicago," Dekker noted. "I think it showed everyone and ourselves that we could climb out of a

A former Chicago Bulls ball boy at the United Center, Duje Dukan flourished in his old stomping grounds, including a thunderous dunk vs. Michigan.
By Icon Sportswire

Sam Dekker and Wisconsin out-scored Purdue 41-to-16 in the second half and advanced to the 2015 Big Ten Tournament championship game. *By Icon Sportswire*

deficit. We stuck together and got wins. It also proved yet again that a ton of different guys can step up and that we can get wins vs. good teams on a neutral court. We knew to just stay the course and play our basketball. That wins."

"I think those comebacks were good for us," Chicagoland native (Deerfield) Duje Dukan added. "We might have needed that."

For Dukan, Friday's opening win was an individual comeback as well.

The son of a Bulls executive, Dukan had long dreamed of competing on the United Center court. Well, competing as a player, that is. Dukan served as a longtime ball boy for the Chicago Bulls, shagging rebounds and mopping sweat for legends like Michael Jordan, Scottie Pippen and his personal favorite, family friend Toni Kukoc.

So here was Dukan, now a 23-year old contributor for the top-seeded Badgers, about to live out his fantasies.

"The United Center is kind of like the mecca of basketball for me," Dukan smiled. "Getting the chance to play there was a dream come true and I really wanted to take advantage of that opportunity and take care of business and win a championship."

Instead, Dukan would miss his first three shots against Michigan and sit scoreless at halftime. Midway through the second half, the Badgers still trailed the Wolverines and consecutive turnovers would send Kaminsky to the bench.

When Wisconsin needed him most, Dukan broke out of his mini-slump. After a UW timeout, the fifth-year graduate student swished a 3-pointer to knot the game at 44-all. Two minutes later, Dukan connected again from distance. Before he was finished, the 6-foot-10 forward slashed to the rim and threw down a ferocious two-handed dunk that sent the Wisconsin bench into euphoric disbelief.

"It was an unbelievable experience," Dukan said looking back. "Having friends and family there and being home was a big part of my personal success. That was a great opportunity for me to help our team pull out some big wins."

Dukan would ride that confidence, chipping in 11 points two days later against Michigan State and going 6-for-12 from 3-point range over the three-game stretch.

"Two years before when we played at the United Center for the conference tournament, Duje and I were both sitting out as redshirts," Gasser remembered. "That whole tournament he just kept saying, 'I can't wait for our senior year when we get to play here. So he waited two years for that chance. He was really excited and gave us a huge lift."

In Saturday's semifinal, the Badgers would face a tough-minded Purdue team that had given Wisconsin all it wanted at the Kohl Center earlier that season. So you can imagine the concern among the Badgers faithful when Wisconsin trailed by five at intermission and clung to a two-point lead with just under 11 minutes remaining.

Instead of watching Purdue pull off the upset, the predominantly red and white United Center crowd witnessed just how powerful the Badgers could be when they flexed their muscles. Over the next four-and-a-half minutes, Wisconsin scored 13 consecutive points, turning a 46-44 nail-biter into a 59-44 laugher. The Badgers' demoralizing run came from every direction: a Kaminsky jumper, a pair of Dekker dunks, a triple from Gasser and free throws from Bronson Koenig and Zak Showalter. The team that had set offensive efficiency records during the regular season had turned up the tempo and turned in a 71-51 spanking.

After shooting just 37 percent in the first half, UW couldn't miss in the second half,

hitting 57 percent. Purdue was the opposite, seeing its 50-percent shooting and 35 first-half points shrivel to 24 percent and 16 points after the recess.

Tucked into the United Center bowels, Dekker was asked in the postgame press conference what was more fun for this team, offense or defense? Knowing his defensive-minded head coach was sitting a few chairs to his right, Dekker played it diplomatically.

"When we're playing defense well, it becomes really fun, because then you can see what it does to us," Dekker hinted behind a wry smile. "When we get those good stops and good momentum, we get our athletes out in the open court and we can make it tough on them and get them on their heels. When we're doing it on the defensive end, it makes offense more fun because one thing leads to another, and we have the guys that can get it done on both ends."

Minutes later, in the privacy of backstage, Dekker would sing a slightly different refrain.

"You have no idea how hard that question was for me to answer. I mean, did that guy know who he was asking?" the notoriously offensive-minded Dekker laughed.

In the ensuing championship game, Dekker and the Badgers would need every ounce of offense and defense.

A few days prior to departing for the Big Ten tournament, Bo Ryan sat in his home office talking with Michigan State head coach Tom Izzo about the regular season that had just completed and the approaching postseason. As he hung up the phone and wished his nemesis-turned-respected adversary good luck, Ryan couldn't help but think, "We're going to play those guys again. We're going to play them in the Big Ten tournament."

In order for a meeting with the third-seeded Spartans to materialize, Michigan

TODAY A

WILL BE CROWN

82

By Brandon Harrison

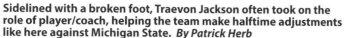

Sidelined with a broken foot, Traevon Jackson often took on the role of player/coach, helping the team make halftime adjustments like here against Michigan State. *By Patrick Herb*

State would have to navigate a treacherous path through No. 6 Ohio State and No. 2 Maryland on the opposite side of the bracket. After pulling off a 62-58 upset over the Terrapins in the second Saturday semifinal, the title bout Ryan forecasted was set.

It would not disappoint.

A Kaminsky 3-pointer in the closing seconds of the first half minimized the early damage for Wisconsin, who retreated to the halftime locker room trailing MSU by one. The championship chess match had produced

seven ties and five lead changes in the opening 20 minutes.

As the Badgers settled into their halftime locker room positions, three rows of chairs neatly facing a dry-erase board, senior Traevon Jackson took up a post at the front of the room. Before Ryan and the UW coaches entered, Jackson – who was still out of action with a broken foot sustained two months earlier – drew a half court diagram and began illustrating what he had observed.

"We're not spacing enough off ball screens," Jackson coached while pointing at his black scribbles. "The way they defend, this guy needs to give enough room so they can't help off. If we give room for the guy coming off the screen, we can get to the rim."

"Trae had a lot of moments during halftime where he'd see something out on the floor and go up to the grease board and draw it," Nigel Hayes explained. "Or he'd say, 'Ok, since we found out that this worked, then we'll take this play and put a variation on it.' Then we'd go out and run it, and we had a lot of success doing that. Several times we closed a half slowly scoring-wise, but we'd take those adjustments or things Coach Ryan noted and it would click in the second half."

In this instance, things didn't click right away for the Badgers. It was Michigan State that came out on the attack. By the time Brandon Dawson converted a turnover into a breakaway dunk, the Spartans had built an 11-point lead with 7:45 remaining.

As the Badgers faced their largest deficit of the season, seemingly everyone in the decidedly red crowd of 17,213 could see UW's Big Ten championship slipping away. Everyone except the Badgers themselves.

"It was frustrating when we dug ourselves that hole," Kaminsky said after the game. "They were taking advantage of us and we weren't responding. It was about us turning up the energy level and having some pride. But we knew we could do it. We never wavered."

Koenig snapped a near four-minute scoring drought with a 3 from the top of the key, but credit Kaminsky with one of the major turning points. Down 59-49,

Kaminsky spun baseline and powered through Dawson for a two-handed dunk plus a foul. Kaminsky's three-point play was the start of a scoring flurry that featured a Hayes circus-like and-one, as well as treys from Koenig and Kaminsky.

In a flash of brilliance, the Badgers had battled from the brink and electrified a pro-Wisconsin crowd in an environment that would rival any NCAA tournament atmosphere.

"It was awesome," Kaminsky boasted of the crowd. "You could hear the difference between the two fan groups. Having that loud of fans when you're trying to make a run is very, very good because they do factor into the game. Without our fans there, maybe things don't go the same."

UW had fought back, but still trailed 69-67 after a difficult Travis Trice runner with 44 seconds left in regulation. After a 30-second timeout, Koenig would misfire on a 3, with the long rebound caroming toward the sideline.

Cue Captain America.

Gasser tracked down the loose ball, throwing it backwards over his head as he leaped head-first into the courtside press table.

"It was just one of those plays where there was 20 seconds left and it's a championship game," Gasser said, downplaying his efforts. "I would always tell the guys to value every single possession and do whatever it takes to win. So I have to live that way too. I can't tell them to do that and then not throw my body around."

Gasser's blind save fell into the hands of MSU's Denzel Valentine, who instinctually turned to fire an outlet pass that Dekker intercepted near midcourt, giving the Badgers new life.

"I was upside down and kind of under the tables," Gasser went on. "I remember saying to one of the media guys, 'Do we have the ball?' Then they kind of picked me up and threw me back over the table and onto the court. I remember for a split second being open in the corner and thinking, 'If I get this, I'm shooting it. I deserve to shoot it.' I didn't end up touching it, which is probably a good thing because I was a little banged up."

Instead, Koenig was fouled on a drive to the basket, giving him two free throws with 15.2 seconds to play. The sophomore point guard calmly knocked down both shots to tie the game at 69-all.

Replays would later show that Gasser's foot was actually on the out-of-bounds line when he jumped for the decisive save. But the footwork went unnoticed and after Dawson's baseline jumper rattled out at the buzzer, Wisconsin had forced the first-ever overtime in a Big Ten tournament championship.

"When I saved it, I knew I was out," Gasser confessed. "I saw my foot on the line. But for some reason I also knew they weren't going to call it. By the time I got up and saw what was going on, Bronson had the ball. So I thought I had saved it and he

Nigel Hayes (right) and Bronson Koenig (left) opened the overtime period with back-to-back 3-pointers and helped the Badgers polish off the championship. *By Kamil Krzaczynski*

By Scott Boehm

caught it. I didn't know until the next day that Valentine turned it over."

"It didn't surprise me at all that he was the guy to make that play," Dekker admired. "He would sacrifice everything to win. That was his role and his leadership and he wore it well. You need that out of a leader. You need

that to win championships."

Gasser's sideline heroics would overshadow his even more impressive defensive effort on Trice. MSU's leading scorer, the senior guard was limited to six points on 2-for-8 shooting with four turnovers.

In the extra session, Hayes – who finished with a game-high 25 points, including a 12-for-12 performance at the foul line – started the scoring with a 3-pointer at the shot clock buzzer. Two possessions later Koenig knocked down his fourth triple of the game and Wisconsin was on its way to an 80-69

WISCONSIN BADGERS 2015 BIG TEN MEN'S BASKETBALL TOURNAMENT CHAMPIONS

WISCONSIN BADGERS 2015 BIG TEN MEN'S BASKETBALL TOURNAMENT CHAMPIONS

86

win, securing its first Big Ten championship since 2008.

The Badgers shut out Michigan State in overtime, forcing the Spartans into 0-for-6 shooting in the extra period and leaving Izzo shaking his head.

"I thought we played one of the greatest games we've played for 32, 32-and-a-half minutes, or 35, 36 minutes. And then we made a couple mistakes, and they made a couple of great shots, and that's the way the game goes," Izzo said.

"That was a high-level NCAA tournament game right there, if you ask me," Ryan noted. "As far as the crowd, the intensity, the swings, the up-and-down."

When the clock struck zero, the Badgers were again the team left standing.

They bounced and yelled at midcourt, they wore championship shirts and hats, they took selfies. Tournament MVP Kaminsky tried to catch the falling confetti like a snowflake on his tongue and for the second time in two weeks, they marched up a ladder and snipped pieces of their championship net.

"I really enjoyed that game," Hayes acknowledged. "Growing up and as a competitor, I always wanted those moments where you're the one making things happen in a big game. During the game I was able to step outside of myself and I was basically watching myself play and saying to myself, 'Man, isn't this what you always talked about? Hitting big shots, getting big rebounds, big free throws to win games and pumping up the crowd?' Basically I got outside of myself and could appreciate that this is what I always talked about and wanted."

"That was definitely one of my favorite games of the year," Gasser added. "To play for a championship, to be down and somehow come back and win a nail-biter, that's a game I'll never forget."

Minutes later the Badgers gathered in a United Center lounge to watch the NCAA tournament Selection Show. For the first time in history, Wisconsin would hear CBS anchor Greg Gumbel proclaim the following words, "The Badgers... have earned the right to a number one seed."

Wisconsin had claimed the pole position in the West Region of the bracket.

"Being the first team in school history to get a number one seed was pretty neat," Ryan admitted. "I never pay much attention to that kind of thing, but that's a sign of respect and means you've done some pretty good things."

Long after the confetti had been swept and the lights dimmed, Kaminsky, Hayes and Koenig exited the press conference and walked across the quiet United Center court on their way back to the locker room. At the same time, CBS announcers Jim Nantz, Bill Raftery and Grant Hill were finishing up a live hit for the Selection Show and the Badgers trio stopped to say their goodbyes.

As they walked off the floor together, Hill asked, "What do you guys think of your draw? Looks tough, you'd have to play Kentucky in the Final Four."

Without letting the others speak, Kaminsky jumped in, "Mr. Hill, we want Kentucky." ∎

◄ After they secured Wisconsin's second-ever Big Ten tournament championship, Bo Ryan and the Badgers made history and earned the school's first-ever No. 1 seed in the NCAA tournament. *By Patrick Gorski | Cal Sport Media*

CAPTAIN AMERICA

"Gasser's true value isn't measured on a stat sheet or record book."

At Wisconsin's season-ending reception at the Kohl Center, Nigel Hayes and his teammates reclined on a temporary stage watching a series of videos that featured poignant moments of the season. When the tape turned to Josh Gasser's heroic dive over one of the media tables to save a ball and set up the Badgers' game-tying points in the Big Ten championship game, Hayes leaned back and slowly shook his head.

"See, that's why we're going to miss him," Hayes whispered to no one in particular. "Who else is going to make a play like that? That's 'Clutch Josh.' That's 'Captain America.' That's my hero."

Josh Gasser was at Wisconsin long enough to earn a lot of nicknames. He deserved every one of them.

In the summer of 2014, fellow senior Frank Kaminsky penned a blog filling out a baseball lineup with players from the hoops team. His easiest selection was placing Gasser at shortstop.

"Josh is Captain America. I really don't need to say much else besides saying he is our leader. Josh is like Derek Jeter in the manner that he is popular amongst his peers. It is hard to find someone that hates Jeter, just like it is hard to find someone who hates Josh Gasser."

From that day forward, the nickname "Captain America" stuck. The moniker fits Gasser as well as Gasser fits Wisconsin basketball.

In the history of the program, you'd be hard pressed to find a player who epitomized Wisconsin's toughness, work ethic, leadership, courage and skill more than Josh Gasser.

A native of Port Washington, Gasser always dreamed of playing for the Badgers. As an 8-year old in 2000, he watched Wisconsin's improbable run to the Final Four, mesmerized by the team's defensive-minded floor leader, Mike Kelley.

A two-sport athlete who excelled in football as much as basketball, Gasser wasn't heavily recruited entering the summer before his senior season. The Badgers had kept tabs on him, but the first time Ryan laid eyes on the slender guard was at an AAU tournament in July.

"A lot of my former players who were in the Milwaukee area who had seen him play some high school and AAU ball knew he was a good athlete and a tough competitor. We went to see him play at a tournament – I think he knew I was in the stands because he scored like 15 of his team's first 20 points until he drove one time and sprained his ankle so badly that he couldn't even come back and play football that fall. But I could see some things he was doing and how tough he was playing. The team he was playing was pretty good and he took no step back from anyone or anything."

Two weeks later, Ryan offered him a scholarship. Passing up offers from Northwestern and Northern Iowa, for Gasser, the decision was easy.

When Gasser stepped on campus in Madison, Ryan recognized he would fit right in.

"He wasn't one of those young colts that is still growing when they get on campus," Ryan explained. "He came in with hair on his legs. At 18 years old, Josh was pretty much the same person he was at 22. Aside from adding strength, his maturity and attitude were ready the day he arrived."

So confident in Gasser, Ryan inserted him into the starting lineup in just the second game of his freshman season, an 85-53 win over North Dakota. In Ryan's first nine seasons in Madison only two other players had started as true freshmen, NBA first-round draft picks Devin Harris and Alando Tucker.

The role wasn't too big for Gasser.

It took Gasser 19 games to do something no one else in the history of Wisconsin men's basketball had accomplished, producing the first triple-double in UW's 113-year history. In a January 23, 2011 runaway win at Northwestern, Gasser tallied 10 points, 12 rebounds and 10 assists to post the first triple-double by a Big Ten freshman since Magic Johnson in 1977.

Exactly one month later, at Michigan, he was recording another first.

Trailing by two in the final seconds at Crisler Arena in Ann Arbor, Gasser received a pass from teammate Jordan Taylor, who was trapped on the perimeter. With 1.4 seconds on the clock, Gasser let it fly from just right

By John Fisher | Cal Sport Media

of the top of the arc. The ball caromed off the backboard as the buzzer sounded and dropped straight through the net for a 53-52 win. Almost uncertain of what to do next, Gasser looked around wide-eyed before getting tackled and mobbed at center court.

"What was funny about my freshman year is, I never set out to make headlines or anything, I just wanted to work my tail off and do anything asked of me to help the team," Gasser admitted. "There were a lot of people who didn't think I could make it at UW. I just wanted to prove I belonged."

Mission accomplished.

Over five seasons in Madison, Gasser would become one of the most respected players in the nation.

"Josh had a leadership by example that you can't replace," Sam Dekker admired. "There are guys like him on other teams, but you don't fully appreciate what he brings until you have a guy like him in your circle. His contributions didn't always show up in the box score, but he always won games with leadership, defense, toughness. He is one of those dogs you need to pull the sled."

Gasser's toughness was tested in the fall of 2012. Anointed the team's starting point guard after the graduation of Taylor, an All-American, Gasser tore apart his left knee during preseason practice on October 27.

He would endure a grueling 12-month rehabilitation, but returned to the court in 2013 hardly missing a beat. On November 8, Gasser scored a team-high 19 points in the season-opening win over St. John's. You would expect nothing less from Captain America.

"The way he attacked his rehab and the example he showed really rubbed off on his teammates," Ryan said.

"The thing I admire most about Josh is his sacrifice," Nigel Hayes revered. "In all aspects. He sacrificed his stats, he sacrificed his body. When I joke around about, 'We

Even as a freshman alongside All-Americans Jon Leuer (30) and Jordan Taylor (with ball), Josh Gasser played a vital role for the Badgers. *By David Stluka*

couldn't do this or that without Josh,' it's in the most literal sense. We'll find that out quickly next year if we don't replace him with a lockdown defender and a leader."

"Most people wouldn't put themselves through the physical toll he did," Kaminsky added. "But that was Josh's role and he loved it and embraced it. That's what made us such a good team, having a leader that day-in-and-day-out pushed his body to the limit to make our team better."

Always the first to dive on the floor, or over a scorer's table, Gasser took pride in his toughness.

"I probably get my toughness from watching Brett Favre," Gasser laughed. "He

was my hero."

So you imagine his excitement when the Packers legend left him a minute-long voicemail on his birthday. Turns out Gasser's sister, Lauren, reached out to Favre and orchestrated the gift. Devastated that he missed the call, Gasser tried calling the number back but to no avail.

"I kept my phone on me every second and even had somebody hold it during practice in case he called back," Gasser laughed. "But at least I've got the voicemail saved. That's a keeper."

Much like his hero Favre, longevity will be one of Gasser's lasting legacies.

Two nights before taking on Kentucky,

each of the remaining teams assembled at the Hilbert Circle Theatre in Indianapolis for the annual Final Four Salute, ringing in the crowning weekend. At the event hosted by the CBS broadcast crew of Jim Nantz, Bill Raftery and Grant Hill, it is custom to pass the official game ball out to one player from each team in the audience.

When it was Wisconsin's turn to touch the hallowed rock, the 71-year old Raftery needled, "I want to give it to the only player as old as me, that's why I'm passing it to Josh Gasser."

You can excuse Raftery and nearly everyone else making old man jokes at Gasser's expense.

The homegrown kid who just wanted to prove he could hang in at his state's flagship university, Gasser set UW career service records in every category possible. He played 4,774 minutes in 148 games, including 144 starts. His teams reached the Sweet 16 or better in each of his four healthy seasons as he accumulated a program-record 17 NCAA tournament starts. More importantly to him, only two players in Big Ten history – Ohio State's David Lighty (129) and Aaron Craft (119) – played in more wins than Gasser's 117.

"Of all the stats, the one I'm most proud of is wins," Gasser said. "That's what I'll remember. And that's what I'd want to be remembered for."

He'll be remembered for a lot. One of the more well-rounded players in team annals, Gasser graduated from UW as a 1,000-point scorer but also a three-time selection to the Big Ten All-Defensive Team. Gasser finished with one of the top assist-to-turnover marks in Badgers history but also ranks among the school's top 10 3-point shooters with a career mark of 40 percent.

But to his teammates, Gasser's true value isn't measured on a stat sheet or record book.

"You can't pinpoint one area where Josh had his biggest impact," Duje Dukan commented. "Collectively, he affected the whole team. Off the court, he provided that leadership and mature voice. On the court, we counted on his experience, leadership and competitive edge. He made the little plays that didn't necessarily show up in the box score. He could put up impressive stats, but numbers would never be a good indication of how valuable he was."

"Josh does everything on the court that you may never realize is happening," Kaminsky agreed. "But at the end of the game when you look back and see all the things that he did and how he changed so many plays, you're kind of shocked about it. His willingness to do anything that needs to be done for a team makes him somebody you want out on the court at all times."

Sports Illustrated's Seth Davis made him a repeat pick to his All-Glue Team, an annual list that recognizes college basketball's "unheralded but invaluable players." The description for the honor could have served as Gasser's biography:

"A Glue Guy is tricky to spot and hard to define. It's not enough for him to be willing to do all the proverbial little things that don't show up on a stat sheet. He must do those things enthusiastically.

Playing good defense, setting hard screens, making the extra pass, diving on the floor to win 50–50 balls—all these things are vital components in winning. Few players are willing to do them. The Glue Guy is willing to emphasize them."

Captain America did those things. Every game, every practice.

"Everybody respected Josh for how he played the game," Ryan said. "He did all the little things every day and that's why watching him was so rewarding. He never took a possession off in practice. If he's doing a shooting drill, it's the most important thing in his life at that time. If he's doing a passing drill, that next pass he's making is going to be his best.

"I've had a few players like that in my career, but it's uncommon. And when you do have one like that, you make sure they know they're appreciated." ∎

"Most people wouldn't put themselves through the physical toll he did. But that was Josh's role and he loved it and embraced it. That's what made us such a good team." – Frank Kaminsky *By David Stluka*

THE DANCE BEGINS

"This team wants to make history."

In the 1850s, the city of Omaha, Nebraska, earned the nickname "Gateway to the West" from settlers looking to cross the Missouri River, many on their way to California.

The Badgers traveled to Omaha with the same design in mind.

Carrying the banner as the first No. 1 seed in program history, Wisconsin would take on No. 16 Coastal Carolina in Friday's opening round of the 2015 NCAA Tournament.

Well aware of the fact that historically a 16 seed had never taken out a 1 seed, the Badgers had varying degrees of acknowledgement.

"Crazy things always happen in the NCAA tournament and someday a 16 will beat a 1, you know it will," Josh Gasser would say. "This team wants to make history, but not in that way."

Frank Kaminsky took a different approach: "It's not a thought at all in my mind. Once you think it, it enters your mind and then it makes it real and it makes it a possibility. So I'm not even going to think about it."

As a 16 seed just one year earlier, Coastal Carolina had nearly pulled off the miracle, leading top-seeded Virginia 35-30 at halftime. Virginia would go on to win, but the memory stuck with the Chanticleers and gave them confidence for the matchup with

Wisconsin, even if it was a little misguided.

"I played against Josh Gasser a couple of times in AAU," CCU senior guard and Racine native Josh Cameron said before the game. "I really went at him a lot and did well. I like the matchup."

In addition to history (No. 1 seeds were a combined 120-0 against 16s), the Badgers also had Greg Gard on their side. Among the countless things Wisconsin basketball has become very good at, is winning its opening game of the NCAA tournament. With Gard, the team's associate head coach, in charge of the first-round scouting reports, the Badgers are an impressive 12-2 in tournament lid-lifters.

On this occasion, the scouting report could have offered little else but instructions to feed Wisconsin's three-headed frontcourt monster of Kaminsky, Sam Dekker and Nigel Hayes. Without a starter taller than 6-foot-7, Coastal Carolina had no ability to slow the trio.

Kaminsky recorded his 12th double-double of the season, making it look easy at times with 27 points and 12 rebounds. Dekker scored 20 points and Hayes contributed another 14 as the Badgers racked up 40 points in the paint and coasted to an 86-72 win.

Wisconsin's interior domination seemed to fuel the outside game as well. The Badgers knocked down 11 triples in a game that was never closer than 11 points in the second half.

"We tried everything," Chanticleers coach Cliff Ellis said after the game, echoing a sentiment many UW opponents had voiced during the season. "We pressed, we zoned, we manned. Nothing stopped them."

"Frank was big that night, like he was all season," Dekker said, looking back. "Across the board we had a lot of guys step up. The NCAA tournament can be a grind, especially when you turn around

The trio of Sam Dekker, Nigel Hayes and Frank Kaminsky combined for 61 points, carrying the Badgers to an easy opening-round win over Coastal Carolina. *By Icon Sportswire*

Hayes and Wisconsin improved to 12-2 in the opening round of the NCAA tournament under Bo Ryan. *By Nati Harnik*

and play again two days later. You'd like to have a game or two like that where it's not as taxing and you can get everybody into the game."

In game two, the taxing UW avoided in game one would come calling like an IRS auditor.

In 2014, Oregon had Wisconsin on the ropes, and it took a big home crowd-fueled comeback in Milwaukee for UW to advance. The Badgers would have no such advantage in the 2015 rematch, but they again found themselves in a second-half fight.

The game pitted two high-powered offenses against each other, as well as a pair of conference MVPs in Kaminsky and Oregon's dynamic scorer and Pac-12 Player of the Year Joe Young. A year earlier, Young lit up the Badgers for 29 points in Wisconsin's win; he would again be the Ducks' spark plug in the second go-around.

With Gasser chasing him all around Omaha,

Young was scoreless and 0-for-5 in the opening 10 minutes as the Badgers built a 20-9 lead. Kaminsky and Hayes again did the heavy lifting early with a combined 13 points.

"We got off to a really good start and felt comfortable early on," Gasser remembered. "But you're not going to hold a great scorer like Young, a high-volume shooter, down forever. We knew he'd get going at some point and we'd have to dig in."

Gasser was right; with 9:23 remaining in the first half Young would connect on a 3-pointer and let out a frustrated roar. By the time the teams retreated to the locker rooms for halftime, Young had 14 points and Wisconsin's lead was down to just three.

Dekker, who had just three points at intermission, came alive in the second half. On the second possession of the period, Hayes found Dekker open on the wing for a 3-pointer, seemingly jump-starting the 6-foot-9 forward.

◀ Wisconsin vs. Oregon provided a matchup of conference players of the year in Kaminsky and Joe Young. *By Icon Sportswire*

▼ Dekker led the Badgers with 17 points vs. the Ducks, including 14 in the second half. *By Nati Harnik*

"The only thing that matters in the NCAA tournament is getting wins," Dekker recognized. "Pretty or ugly, it's a win and you're on to the next game. That Oregon game was a tight one, but I think that was good for us. It got us into the mindset that we're going to face tight games down the stretch and it's not going to be easy."

The Badgers' depth, which had been a concern all season, continued to rise to the occasion. Building off Duje Dukan's breakout Big Ten tournament, this time it was

"We didn't play our best in Omaha. But we earned the right to go back to work. That's all we can ask for." Josh Gasser
By Icon Sportswire

sophomore Zak Showalter's turn. The reserve guard connected on a 3-pointer and a reverse lay-in during the second half and pulled in five rebounds in 15 productive minutes.

"I knew going into this game Josh and Bronson (Koenig) might get into some foul trouble because Joseph Young is that good of a player," Showalter said from the postgame press conference dais. "So I was prepared. And it felt good to get in the first half, get more comfortable, and then by the second half, I was ready."

Hidden amidst Showalter's stat line was a play that revealed one of the reasons Wisconsin is so good. Every step in practice, every fundamental drill, has meaning and manifests itself at different moments. At nearly every workout you'll find the Badgers running a drill called "Cover-Uncover," designed to make offensive decisions rote

memory. Showalter couldn't help but recognize the situation when he caught the ball near the top of arc with his team clinging to a late three-point lead.

"We'd worked on that drill so many times, where you catch it, ball fake to the corner, and if the defender goes to the corner – which he did – and he leaves me, I'm wide open and ready to take the shot," said Showalter, who had made just one triple all season to that point.

Splash! Assist Bo Ryan.

Oregon, however, wouldn't go away. The Ducks pulled even at 52-all on a 3 from Dwayne Benjamin with 5:54 left to play. As they demonstrated time and again the weekend prior in Chicago, there would be no panic in the Badgers.

"We never flinched," Gasser recollected. "There was a calmness in the huddle during

that second half. No one ever had that 'uh oh' look in their eyes. We'd been in this spot before."

After a Koenig free throw, Dekker finished an up-and-under lay-in at the rim to push UW ahead, 56-52. On the ensuing possession a Gasser steal and outlet pass to a streaking Dekker seemed to set up a back-breaking alley-oop dunk. But a timeout from Ryan on the UW bench thwarted the scoring chance, triggering Gasser to react with an open-palmed pleading to his coach, "Noooo, why?"

Ryan calmed his team down and, as if he knew it all along, installed a play that traded the nullified dunk for a Dekker 3-pointer from the corner. UW would take control and ice the game with free throws down the stretch.

Credit Ryan with two assists.

After the game, Dekker, who finished with a team-high 17 points, put his arm around Ryan and jokingly asked him, "You just wanted me to get a 3 instead of a 2 there, huh? Good call, Coach."

For the fourth time in five seasons, the Badgers were on to the Sweet 16. There were high-fives and congratulatory hugs on the court, but a dissatisfied feeling hung in the white-washed cinder block locker room.

"We expected to win," Gasser would say plainly. "At that point in the year, we were happy with the win, but something was missing. It's hard to pinpoint what, but we all recognized it. We needed to play better. That's what I loved about this team so much, we were never satisfied. We might win games, but we wanted to play well individually and collectively as a team.

"We didn't play our best in Omaha. But we earned the right to go back to work. That's all we can ask for."

Wisconsin was headed to Los Angeles for the West Regional. Having won a day earlier, North Carolina, Xavier and Arizona were already waiting. ∎

SOUNDTRACK: LAUGHTER

"Welcome to the 2015 Wisconsin Badgers: ruthlessly-efficient assassins on the court, delightful misfits off it."

On the eve of the national championship game, Bo Ryan took his perch behind a microphone atop a temporary stage in the Lucas Oil Stadium underbelly-turned-media-center. Flanked by his starting five, from left to right, Bronson Koenig, Frank Kaminsky, Josh Gasser, Sam Dekker and Nigel Hayes, Ryan settled in for a press conference as hundreds of media members sat with pens and cameras at the ready.

The format was the same as the media briefing he and his players had conducted the night before after their scintillating win over Kentucky. It was the same as the press conference they'd participated in the day before that and the one the day before that. In total, over four postseason weekends, Ryan and company had endured no fewer than 16 press conferences in four cities. The monotony could be suppressing.

Or not.

Before the first question was even uttered, the five Badgers players were all trying – and failing – to cover their full-toothed grins. Dekker was whispering something into Hayes' ear, barely able to keep his voice down through the laughter. Gasser and Koenig were doubled over, peaking around Kaminsky both struck with the same "did you see that?" look, Kaminsky shaking his head in joking disapproval.

On the grandest stage of college athletics, on the precipice of the biggest game of their

Wisconsin press conferences became must-see events throughout the NCAA tournament. **By Icon Sportswire**

lives, here were the Badgers, giggling like they had just made eyes with a pretty girl.

Maybe they had. Or maybe they had seen something as mundane as a reporter with his shoe untied. Or maybe they were recounting an absurd video game battle from that morning. There was no telling what was behind those mischievous smiles. The only certainty was that they were having fun.

Against a backdrop of sincere answers and respect for their upcoming opponent, the next 30 minutes unfolded rapt with comedic quirkiness. Dekker peeled his paper NCAA water cup to fashion a bracelet, Kaminsky made faces into a small mounted camera affixed to the table in front of him, Hayes lounged with his size 15 shoes peeking through the black table skirting while

By Mark J. Terrill

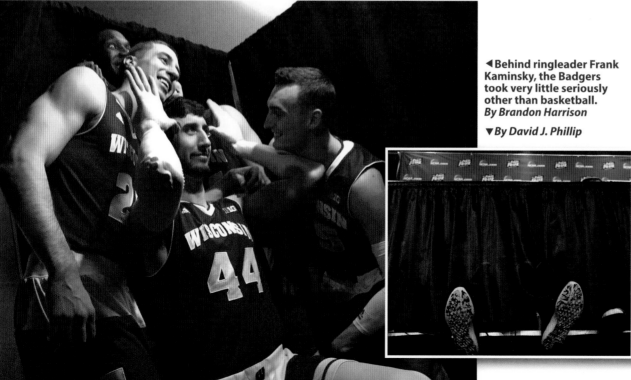

◀ Behind ringleader Frank Kaminsky, the Badgers took very little seriously other than basketball.
By Brandon Harrison

▼ By David J. Phillip

playfully interjecting, "I don't really know how to answer questions, I just thought I was brought here to say some words and you guys might laugh." (More on Hayes' stenographer-teasing wordplay in a bit.)

These are the Badgers, laughing when Kaminsky's voice cracked during a response, trying to keep a straight face as Gasser leans his nose closer and closer to their face or scanning the crowd and then busting up like 12-years olds who had just heard the word "fart."

All the while, with the smirk of a parent watching his children play in the mud, the coach they call "Pops" is basking in his players' revelry.

You could say this press conference was off the rails, but could you be certain there was ever a track to begin with?

If this was how they acted in public, during the most pressure-packed moments of their careers, you should have seen them away from the lights and the cameras.

Amidst a soundtrack of laughter, they bounced their way through the NCAA tournament like it was one big trampoline. Welcome to the 2015 Wisconsin Badgers: ruthlessly-efficient assassins on the court, delightful misfits off it.

◆◆◆◆

"I heard a story once about a boxer or a UFC fighter who came out to the face-off right before the fight and tried to flex every muscle he could so that he looked big and tough," Hayes said after the season. "Then when the fight started he let go of his muscles and he had no energy left and got knocked out immediately. If a person were to try to flex every muscle in his body, eventually they would get to the point where they would pass out.

"That kind of relates to a team in basketball. If your team is uptight and tense

Make 'Em Believe | 99

all the time, eventually you will burn out. That's why you need to relax and not flex your muscles all the time, like our team did off the court. Then when it was time to get on the court, it's all business."

Hayes' quirky, yet astute analogy in itself is an illustration of the Badgers: smart and perceptive enough to understand the moment, yet goofy and grounded enough to see the humor in it.

Fitting that Hayes is the theorist who can explain the phenomena, because he just might be the instigator that sent the Badgers down this rabbit hole of silliness.

"People say we have a loose team and there is no doubt Nigel is a huge part of that. His relationship with Coach Ryan might have started it," Gasser admitted.

You could see it coming. When Ryan made a visit to Hayes' home in Toledo, Ohio, he was struck by his intelligence and his dry wit sense of humor.

"Nigel knows how to make people feel comfortable," Ryan said. "It seems like his mission in life is geared toward making people feel good. But then when he competes, his sole purpose is to try to make people look bad on the other team. The fact that he's on our team... that's pretty good."

From the day he arrived on campus, Hayes's relationship with Ryan has been a little different.

"Nigel's relationship with Coach Ryan is something I had never seen before," Gasser admitted. "When I came in as a freshman and the way most people come in, I don't want to say they're scared of Coach, but you respect him so much that you aren't going to talk back or, when he walks into a room, you're going to snap to attention and almost hold your breath. On the first day, Nigel came in and started making jokes with Coach. He would say things to him that I would never think to say to him, even as a junior and a leader of the team.

From the day he arrived on campus, Nigel Hayes had a different relationship with Bo Ryan, the man he affectionately calls "Pops." *By Andy Manis*

"Nigel has this weird confidence and personality that I think translated to the whole team. Once we saw that a freshman was joking around with Coach, calling him 'Dad' and Coach loving it... it made Coach looser and I think it made our whole team looser."

Ryan noticed it, too.

"During his freshman year I saw him in the gym early one morning all by himself dribbling a basketball in one hand and a tennis ball in the other," Ryan narrated. "The next day I saw him and said, 'Nigel, I didn't want to interrupt your workout, but I saw you out there. Early bird gets the worm.' He answered, 'Yeah, but Coach, did you know that the second mouse always gets the cheese?' I thought, 'Wow, that's one I haven't heard before and I've been around a long time."

Hayes had a unique way of diffusing tense moments. At one January practice during his

The Badgers had an incredible ability to separate focus and fun, like their go-karting excursion in Omaha.
By Patrick Herb

freshman season, Ryan was barking about consecutive turnovers he had just witnessed. Ryan's full-throated yell startled the quiet gym like a jackhammer in church. Hayes, a 6-foot-8, 235-pound forward, turned to Ryan and deadpanned, "See Coach, if you let me play point guard this won't happen."

Ryan couldn't help crack a smile. Tension cut, practice resumed.

"There were little things during film study," Gasser added. "Coach might get on him for not boxing out or something and

Nigel would just blurt out, 'Yep, my bad Coach. I'm an idiot,' and just say something back to him. You don't understand – people don't say anything during film session. But he would make a joke and get everyone to laugh and then refocus. Not everyone can get away with that, but Coach Ryan trusts Nigel and knows he's smart and it comes from a good place."

Hayes' colorful personality made him a fan – and media – favorite during the 2014 NCAA Tournament as he starred in a series of

wildly popular "Hayes for Days" videos. Hayes would pepper his teammates and coaching staff with ridiculous questions as his alter-ego "Nigel Burgundy," named after Will Ferrell's character Ron Burgundy in the hit movie *Anchorman*.

It was Hayes who suggested the team go to a go-kart track the night the Badgers arrived in Omaha for the opening rounds of the NCAA tournament. It was Hayes who tried to interview Kentucky coach John Calipari two days before the Badgers took on the Wildcats in 2014 Final Four. It was Hayes who attached his name to a lawsuit challenging the NCAA's amateur model. It was Hayes who once asked reporters, "Why can't you hear a pterodactyl go to the bathroom? Because the 'p' is silent."

With Hayes around, you always have to be on your toes. Just ask the stenographers who staffed the NCAA tournament press conferences.

During the Badgers' postgame press conference following an 86-72 win over Coastal Carolina, Hayes, Kaminsky and Dekker found themselves transfixed on the woman to their right hammering away on what looked like a miniature typewriter as they talked. After the press conference, the stenographer from ASAP Sports asked the three players if they'd like to learn about her steno machine.

Inquisitive as always, the three players – with Ryan in tow – jumped at the chance. Still cloaked in dried sweat, they took turns asking questions and pushing unmarked buttons all the while marveling and howling at the cryptic way combinations of keystrokes could type names and phrases.

The next afternoon, as he walked to the off-day press conference, Hayes was approached by the stenographer's assistant and asked if he'd like to play a joke on the stenographer, Toni Christy. Never one to turn down a chance for a prank, Hayes complied.

He would recite a series of off-the-wall words to test the typist's real-time skills.

As fate would have it, Hayes received the first question of the press conference.

"Before I answer that question," Hayes began, "I'd like to say a few words: Cattywampus, onomatopoeia, and antidisestablishmentarianism."

When the confused reporter asked what that was all about, Hayes offered the following:

"Well, the wonderful lady over there – I think her title is a stenographer, and she does an amazing job of typing words – sometimes if words are not in her dictionary, maybe if I say soliloquy right now, she may have to work a little harder to type the word; or quandary, or zephyr, xylophone, things like that that make her job really interesting."

A bizarre yet entertaining tradition was born. At every subsequent press conference, Hayes would interject lengthy words to stump the stenographer.

As the Badgers kept winning, words like prevaricated, syzygy, prestidigitation, logorrhea and succedaneum entered the NCAA tournament lexicon. In fact, the stunt grew so big that schools with courtroom reporter programs across the country were thanking Hayes for the incredible exposure and enrollment boost he had provided the profession.

"Some of the words I would stumble upon while I was reading at night, or sometimes they were given to me by friends," Hayes said. "I had probably 10,000 words tweeted at me since the whole thing started in Omaha. I never knew where I'd get the inspiration for the words."

Sometimes it was the words Hayes said "off" the microphone that made headlines. Such was the case at a press conference in L.A. when, after discussing his attempt to stump the stenographer, Hayes leaned back and a "hot" microphone broadcast him whispering, "Gosh, she's beautiful."

Embarrassed, a wide-eyed Hayes then asked the assembled media, "Oh, did you hear that?" Realizing he just publicly confessed his adoration for stenographer Debra Bollman – who was seated just off stage – Hayes covered his face in a vain attempt to hide.

The fascination with stenographers began after a press conference in Omaha, but carried on to every site of the NCAA tournament.
By David Stluka and Patrick Herb

"I love Nigel," Gasser said. "Everything he did in press conferences was hilarious. You might think that his teammates would get annoyed by it or think he was seeking attention, but I loved it."

"I think it took one or two goofballs on the team to make everyone act goofy," Kaminsky pointed out. "When you've got a guy like Nigel on the team not taking anything seriously, other than basketball itself, it kind of rubs off on other people and it kind of snowballs from there."

Hayes has enough personality to illuminate an entire team. But the thing about the Badgers was that he was just one of many characters.

"We were a pretty unique team," Dekker understated. "A lot of teams get along well and say they're close, but I'm not sure any are like us. I can confidently say this was the most fun team I've ever been a part of. You'd hear reporters say that they've never been in a locker room like ours. And that was in front of the media. You should have seen us when the door closed behind them. That togetherness and playfulness absolutely played into our success."

This cast of nonconformists included Kaminsky, the national player of the year, leading the team's inside joke of changing the pronunciation of words to sound nothing like the original. "We might see a sign for a federal prison and Frank would shout out, 'Fed-DARE-ul-lee Pri-ZONE.' I'm sure it wasn't funny to anyone else, but we always laughed," Hayes explained.

Or Kaminsky orchestrating a choreographed reaction to the team's name being called as a No. 1 seed on the NCAA Tournament Selection Show, then seductively massaging the team's Big Ten championship trophy on national TV.

Or take Koenig and Vitto Brown, the seemingly quiet underclassmen who stir it up with the best of them. The team used an app on their cell phones to send one another photos, digs and one-liners, with Koenig and Brown all too often bringing the house down with hilarity.

"We love to give each other crap," Koenig confessed. "My roommate would look at our GroupMe chat and just die laughing. There was absolutely no filter."

Then there's Dekker. When Badgers fans on Twitter panicked upon word that their prized forward had suffered a mild knee injury in October, he responded by filming a spoof video. In the shaky video, Dekker filmed himself in a mock hospital bed complete with oxygen mask, IV bag and a battery of tubes and wires as he said, "Hey Badger fans, thanks for all the support, I should be fine in 2-3 years."

That's the thing about this team, they never took anything seriously, except basketball. And sometimes not even that.

"We were different," Hayes expounded. "Even sometimes right before games when one of the guys, like Frank, would try to give a motivational speech, we'd just laugh because we couldn't take him seriously."

The inside jokes that come from

Media covering the Badgers said that when the season ended they would miss Wisconsin press conferences as much as watching the team's "beautiful, perfect offense." *By Mark J. Terrill*

immature college kids spending countless hours together are too many to count.

"You could walk into our locker room literally three or four hours after practice was over and find guys just hanging out," Gasser said.

"We hung out together for literally hours on end, playing video games like FIFA soccer or Super Smash Bros. on Vitto's N64 or playing ping pong or just watching games," Dekker added. "Those are memories I'll remember forever because it was our way of life."

Perhaps the most remarkable part of the Badgers' endearing nonsense was their ability to turn it off.

"It's amazing they can do what they do and still, when it comes to practice, it's 'I'm going to kick your butt, I want you to try to kick mine,'" Ryan offered at one point during the season. "I'm going to get your (best shot) and compete hard and then go into the locker room and argue about who's the best video game player. It's like being a kid again. When we get on the floor or we do anything

basketball-wise, I never have to worry about them. They can separate."

"We never had a problem focusing when it was time to focus," Gasser said. "That was a major strength of this team. Coach told us as long as we could lock in when we were supposed to, he'd let us be who we are."

"If we're all in this thing together, we may as well enjoy the experience," Ryan told his players. "The good ones can separate and I think you guys can. You're good guys who want to savor every moment of this and you're not going to lose the perspective that it's a game. It's competitive, we're competitive, but it's not the end of the world and we're going to enjoy it."

"We were in the spotlight all year because we were in the top five almost all season and I think the media really embraced the goofiness of this team and our outgoing nature," Dekker continued. "I think they liked that we gave them good quotes and good stories. We enjoyed it, too. We didn't try to be too cool for the stage. We just wanted to be us and show what we're like. That was not an act by any means."

One of the team's favorite games that followed them through every step of the journey was pointing out look-a-likes, usually aimed at making ridiculous comparisons to each other or people they knew.

"We entertained ourselves a lot," Hayes

By Brandon Harrison

said. "Most of the time we were laughing at press conferences it was because we were scanning the crowd for look-a-likes. We would point out somebody and whisper a name and then just start laughing. It became a running gag to find the most absurd comparison for Frank. People that looked nothing like him but might have one similar characteristic like shaggy brown hair or being sort of tall. Again, we entertained ourselves."

The Badgers' hijinks also entertained a nation.

As Fox Sports national college basketball writer Reid Forgrave wrote,

When the buzzer sounds on Monday night's championship, it will be tinged with a hint of sadness.

This sadness comes from two places. One is that, no matter the outcome of this potentially great Wisconsin-Duke matchup, we won't get to see this Wisconsin team's beautiful, perfect offense in action ever again.

The other is that we'll never again get to experience the improv comedy act that has been the Badgers' news conferences during their road to Indianapolis.

I'm not sure which one I'll miss more. If I'm being honest, it's probably the news conferences.

Have you ever seen a group of 18-to-22-year-olds having so much damn fun in the pressure-packed atmosphere of the NCAA tournament? Have you ever seen a team's 67-year-old coach serve as the ringleader instead of the party pooper, as Bo Ryan has with this team? Have you ever seen a sports team that looks so serious on the court also look like such a bunch of goofballs off it?

In a world where we take sports far too seriously — where we talk about a game as a do-or-die situation, where we discuss NFL games as if they are warfare, where we dissect every play and every verbal miscue by famous athletes and then complain when they usually give us the most blasé, anodyne quotes possible — shouldn't we lift up this Wisconsin team as much for what it does off the court as for what it does on it?

Yes. Yes we should. The 2014-15 Badgers will be remembered for many things. But above all, they'll be remembered wearing smiles. ∎

SWEET 16: NORTH CAROLINA

"Congrats... see you in L.A."

The night before Wisconsin took on Oregon in the Round of 32, Sam Dekker sat with his teammates in an Embassy Suites hotel room in Omaha keeping tabs on games going on across the NCAA tournament. Dekker was paying close attention to one game in particular. Across the country in Jacksonville, Florida, North Carolina was putting the finishing touches on an 87-78 win over Arkansas, punching the Tar Heels' ticket to the Sweet 16 in Los Angeles.

Dekker quickly tapped out a text message to UNC junior J.P. Tokoto. The short of it?

"Congrats... see you in L.A."

Dekker and company would make good on the promise, outlasting Oregon 72-65 and setting up a Sweet 16 matchup with fourth-seeded North Carolina. As Dekker was sitting in the holding area awaiting the postgame press conference, his cell phone lit up with a message from Tokoto. The short of it?

"Congrats... see you in L.A."

The game would pit two basketball powerhouses against one another, but also serve as a reunion of close friends and former AAU teammates. For years, Dekker and Tokoto, along with Bronson Koenig on occasion, played together on the Wisconsin Playground Warriors travel team. Now they would meet for the first time as opponents.

"J.P. and I became really good friends," Dekker said of Tokoto, who was a three-time all-state selection at Menomonee Falls High School. "Our AAU team had a lot of practices in Milwaukee so I spent countless nights at his house. He would stay at our house too sometimes when we practiced up north. We did that for three years and got really close."

"We just had that tight brotherhood throughout high school, and we've all stayed pretty close," Tokoto added.

Former AAU teammates J.P. Tokoto (13) of UNC and Sam Dekker had been looking forward to this matchup for quite some time. *By David Stluka*

With their late game vs. Oregon, the Badgers arrived in Madison in the wee hours of Monday morning, 1:40 a.m. to be precise. Already a day behind with North Carolina having played on Saturday, Wisconsin made the decision to fly to California earlier than planned. The Badgers would barely be in Madison long enough to do laundry and repack, departing for Hollywood 16 hours after arrival.

"I remember being tired," Dekker noted. "We got out to L.A. late on Monday night, but we were excited. We got out there early and had all week to prepare and lay low. We got a few days to get off our feet a bit and got to recover from the games before and focus on North Carolina."

Extra days on the West Coast also meant additional missed classes and consequently more missed exams. A year earlier the *New York Times* published a terrific story on the Badgers' impressive ability to balance academics and basketball. This season, the Wisconsin players and student managers took a combined 17 exams during their week in California.

In addition to hob-knobbing with Hollywood stars like Will Ferrell and Jerry Ferrara, the extra day gave Wisconsin time to practice twice at the University of Southern California in addition to an hour-long open practice at the Staples Center. It also gave the Badgers time to revel in their proximity to greatness.

Upon being assigned the Lakers' team locker room at the Staples Center, Nigel Hayes boxed out his teammates to secure the locker of 17-time All-Star Kobe Bryant. He proceeded to tweet a photo of himself in front of Bryant's locker and insist, "I will probably sleep in this locker tonight so that way I can absorb Kobe's powers and ability tonight and hopefully it will help me play well."

Koenig took a jab at Hayes and joked on Twitter "In the Lakers Locker Room for practice..... Just pee'd in the urinal my idol @kobebryant goes in!!!! #Blessed"

The Lakers superstar would eventually tweet back a chuckle and message of good

"The toughness (Wisconsin) showed today was really something."
– UNC coach Roy Williams *By David Stluka*

luck. "Would have loved to meet the Mamba, but I'll take it," Hayes said.

Hayes and company needed all the luck they could find.

"Our travel situation was a little weird, basically going straight out to the West Coast, but it allowed us to get our minds and bodies right," Gasser offered. "We were ready to go, we just didn't play well in the first half against UNC."

How the standards at Wisconsin have changed. The Badgers, who had never beaten North Carolina in the history of the program, trailed by just two, 33-31, at the half and, to a man, felt as though they had played poorly.

"We thought that even with the way we shot the ball in the first half, it was still just a one-possession game," Bo Ryan said. "So we felt if we just got back to knocking down shots and make them move a little more on defense, it might affect their offense at the other end. We were standing too much."

Maybe Ryan was right. UW shot just 36 percent, while allowing the Tar Heels to connect on 50 percent on their shots and tally eight fast-break points. Three of the Badgers' top four scorers – Kaminsky, Hayes and Koenig – were a combined 3-for-19 from the field.

A big reason Wisconsin trailed by just two? Sam Dekker was emerging as the star everyone knew he would become.

After scoring 20 and 17 in UW's first two tournament games, Dekker already had 15 points and six boards at the break vs. North Carolina. As the 6-foot-9 junior's confidence grew, so did his willingness to attack. Dekker opened the game with a 3-pointer, but then scored five buckets around the rim, including a tip-in at the halftime buzzer to keep the Badgers within striking distance.

"Sam was one of our difference makers," Gasser explained. "We knew what we'd get out of Frank, Trae (Jackson), Bronson and myself, but in my opinion, Sam and Nigel were the guys that could take us from a really good team to being great. I think you saw that with Sam in the NCAA tournament."

Another heartwarming moment came 5:15

into the game. Senior guard Traevon Jackson, who had not seen game action since breaking his foot on Jan. 11 at Rutgers and was a game time decision as late as the day before, walked to the scorer's table and checked himself in, replacing Koenig. Eight seconds later, Gasser kicked the ball out to an open Jackson in the corner.

"He didn't even hesitate," Gasser smiled thinking back. "Shot it and knocked down a 3. I think that's the happiest I've been on the court in a long time. Knowing how much hard work he put in, I could feel how happy he must have felt and it made me really proud. Those are the type of plays that kind of stick with you forever."

The Staples Center crowd erupted and even Jackson couldn't hide his grin. "I was just happy and grateful to be back out there," he said. "That was a great way to come into the game, and not just for myself, but so my team knew that I wasn't just out there to take up space, I'm here to help."

"Trae was doing what Trae does, having the flair for the dramatic," Dekker marveled. "His first minutes, his first touch, since January and he puts up a 3 and hits it. He got the crowd into it and that really spurred us. It was such a cool moment and the place went crazy. I don't think it was just Wisconsin fans, I think everyone in the gym was like, 'What? This guy hasn't played for how many months and he just did that?'"

"You had to step back and just say, 'Hey this is a pretty good storybook,'" Ryan admired. "It was good for him. He had worked hard."

Jackson's feel-good moment wore off quickly as things were looking bleak for the Badgers at the under 12-minute media timeout of the second half. North Carolina's lead had grown to seven, 53-46, and Kaminsky was headed to the bench after inadvertently being smacked in the eye by UNC's Isaiah Hicks.

After missing the previous 19 games with a broken foot, Traevon Jackson returned vs. the Tarheels and knocked down a 3-pointer just eight seconds after checking into the game. *By David Stluka*

After a Dekker missed 3, a signature Gasser play (see: hustle) prevented the Badgers' deficit from growing even larger.

"Josh made one of the biggest plays of the game when he stripped Tokoto on a fast break opportunity and the ball went out of bounds off Tokoto," Ryan remembered. "We were down seven and it could have gone to nine. We needed that."

Kaminsky re-entered the game and promptly drove and kicked to Koenig for a 3-pointer from the wing. A Kaminsky defensive rebound then led to a three-point play from Hayes at the other end. Game on.

"From my perspective, I remember thinking, 'You're playing North Carolina? This is pretty cool,'" Hayes confessed. "But once we started playing, it was any other game. When we were trailing in the second half of that game there wasn't much that needed to be said. We all just kind of looked at one another and collectively nodded and said 'Alright, now it's time to turn it on.'"

Still trailing by three with just over eight minutes remaining, Wisconsin got a lift from an unlikely source.

"You don't have a season like we had without having multiple contributions and timely contributions like Zak Showalter in that UNC game," Ryan said. "You could see by the bench reaction that his teammates responded to his effort. Without a doubt, Showy gave us a lift."

A reserve guard who averaged just 2.1 points and 7.7 minutes per game, Showalter first scored on a lefty finger roll to pull UW within one. Moments later, Gasser hit Showalter for a backdoor reverse layup to give the Badgers their first lead since the opening minutes of the half. On the very next possession, Showalter picked the pocket of Tar Heels guard Nate Britt and finished the breakaway layup for a 63-60 lead.

"I believe Showy actually turned that game around defensively and offensively," Dekker

By David Stluka

affirmed. "We were in a stretch where we had gone for a while without a basket and he really got us going. Those are the type of plays you need to win games, especially in a Sweet 16. You need everyone to step up and it was Showy that night."

"I told everyone I could, without Showy, we don't win that game," Hayes agreed. "Without him we're probably going home after that."

The game was still in doubt in the final two minutes as a Marcus Paige trey pulled UNC within 69-67, but Dekker had the answer. Working off the right block, Dekker pivoted and scored on a pretty up-and-under, two of his career-high 23 points to go with 10 boards.

The Badgers scored 33 points on their final 19 possessions, going 9-for-13 from the field and hitting 12 of 13 free throws to seal it. UW scored 48 points and shot 57 percent with just two turnovers in the second half. Kaminsky finished with 19 points, 14 coming in the second half, while Hayes added 12.

"The toughness that they showed today was really something," North Carolina coach Roy Williams admired. "It's strange, the difference between winning and losing is so small."

"As a team we knew we'd win," Hayes said matter-of-factly. "People can call that arrogant or cocky, but it's more just a level of confidence and knowing that if we each play our best we can beat any team in the country. We didn't know how we'd win, but we knew we would."

For the fifth time in six postseason games, the Badgers had been on the brink of extinction. For the fifth time in six games, the Badgers had refused to lose.

"Our coaches never waver and it rubs off on us," Dekker avowed. "We never waver." ∎

BADGERS GO HOLLYWOOD

"Frank the Tank meets Frank the Tank."

In 2014, Wisconsin's path to the Final Four took them to Anaheim, California. While the home of Disneyland might be considered part of the greater Los Angeles area, in terms of the Hollywood glitz and glamor, the Badgers might as well have been in Sacramento.

The Badgers' trip to Tinsel Town in 2015 had a completely different feel.

From the moment Wisconsin's draw came up and L.A. was a potential regional destination, an idea was hatched... what if Frank the Tank could meet Frank the Tank?

UW's All-American and resident goofball Frank Kaminsky had developed the nickname Frank the Tank during his high school days at Benet Academy in Lisle, Illinois, and the legend only grew with his remarkable stardom. In fact, the cover of the March 23, 2015 issue of *Sports Illustrated* even pictured Kaminsky standing in front of a retired Army battle tank emblazoned with the words 'FRANK the TANK.'

As legendary as Kaminsky is, no one popularized the Frank the Tank moniker like Hollywood icon Will Ferrell in the blockbuster hit *Old School*. His lovable character, Frank Ricard, is at a crossroads deciding between a life as a responsible adult and family man or embracing the fun-spirited hijinks of his frat-brother, alter-ego "Frank the Tank."

Given Kaminsky's poised yet playful duality, the two Tanks seemed a perfect match. This meeting had to happen.

The Badgers took care of their end of the deal by dispatching Coastal Carolina and Oregon to advance to the regional in L.A. Turns out that was the easy part.

In between games in Los Angeles, the Badgers were treated to a private screening of the movie *Entourage* at the Warner Brothers Studios. *By Patrick Herb*

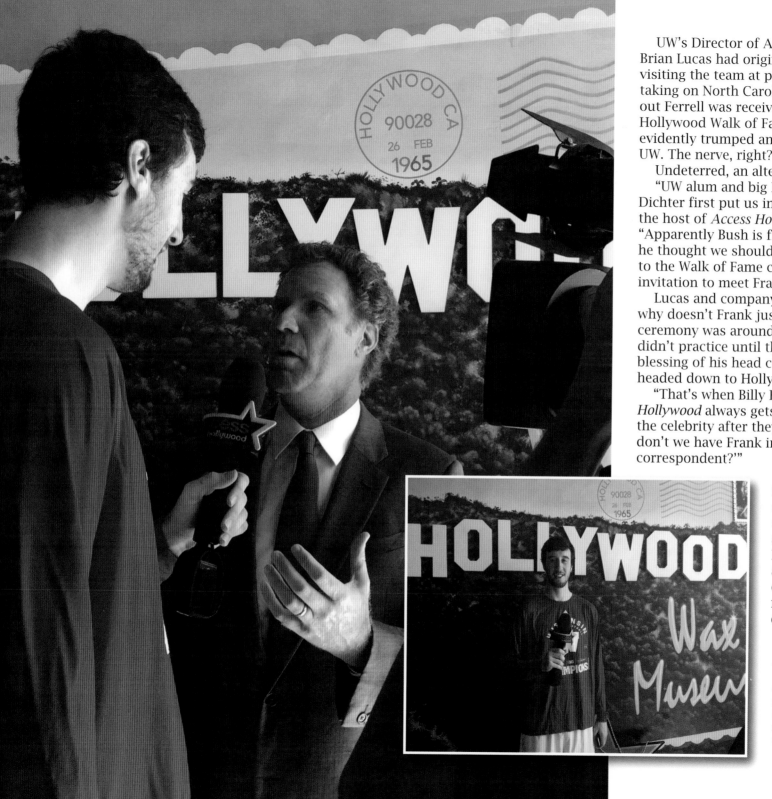

UW's Director of Athletic Communications Brian Lucas had originally dreamed of Ferrell visiting the team at practice the day before taking on North Carolina in the Sweet 16. Turned out Ferrell was receiving his star on the Hollywood Walk of Fame that day, which evidently trumped any little meet-and-greet with UW. The nerve, right?

Undeterred, an alternate plan revealed itself.

"UW alum and big Badgers supporter Kenny Dichter first put us in contact with Billy Bush, the host of *Access Hollywood*," Lucas explained. "Apparently Bush is friends with Will Ferrell and he thought we should send Bucky Badger down to the Walk of Fame ceremony to deliver an invitation to meet Frank and the team."

Lucas and company went one step further: why doesn't Frank just do it himself? The ceremony was around 11 a.m. and the Badgers didn't practice until that afternoon, so with the blessing of his head coach, Kaminsky was headed down to Hollywood.

"That's when Billy Bush said, 'Well *Access Hollywood* always gets the first interview with the celebrity after they receive their star, why don't we have Frank interview Will Ferrell as our correspondent?'"

So there was Kaminsky, inside the security barrier, standing 10 feet from a stage occupied by Ferrell as well as fellow actors Kevin Hart, John C. Reilly and Molly Shannon. A career spent on the receiving end of interview questions, Kaminsky was

Serving as a correspondent for *Access Hollywood*, Frank Kaminsky interviewed Will Ferrell, saying, "I've never been more nervous in my life." .
By Patrick Herb

Actor Jerry Ferrara (blue shirt) and *Entourage* creator Doug Ellin (hat) stopped by the Badgers practice on the USC campus.   *By Brandon Harrison*

preparing to be on the other end of the microphone.

"I've never been so nervous in my whole life," Kaminsky admitted moments before the interview. "I'd be more comfortable playing basketball in front of a million people in my underwear than doing what I'm about to do."

Not knowing how long he had to interview the comedic icon or what kind of format *Access Hollywood* wanted, Kaminsky prepared a few off-the-wall questions like, "Why do Kamikaze pilots wear helmets?"

Kaminsky handled the interview like a seasoned veteran, asking Ferrell to stand back-to-back so he could compare heights. When the 7-footer towered over the 6-foot-3 Ferrell, Kaminsky joked, "Kevin Hart (5-foot-4) asked me to do that so you know how he feels."

Off air, Kaminsky and Ferrell visited for a while and took photos before the comedian signed a copy of the *Sports Illustrated* cover with the words, "Hey Frank – nice name, Will Ferrell."

"Of all the cool stuff I've gotten to do, that one might be the best," Kaminsky gushed after the season. "Although *Entourage* was pretty awesome too."

Just a few hours after rubbing elbows with Ferrell on Hollywood Boulevard, Kaminsky and his teammates were at it again. This time, the Badgers mixed it up with the creator of the hit television show and movie *Entourage*, Doug Ellin, and one of its stars, Jerry Ferrara, who played the character "Turtle." As the team practiced on the campus of USC, the duo dropped by to say hello and get a few shots up with the guys.

They also had a special offer.

Ellin and Ferrara had recently finished production of the widely-anticipated *Entourage* movie and were awaiting the official release on June 3. But they were willing to show the Badgers a private advanced screening at the Warner Brothers studios.

There was one catch. The screening had to be set for Friday, March 27, the day after the Badgers' Sweet 16 showdown with North Carolina. That meant Wisconsin would have to beat the Tar Heels in order to still be in Los Angeles and take advantage of the exclusive showing.

"I'm so glad they didn't tell us about that private screening until after the game," said Kaminsky, a huge fan of the show, who once penned a blog titled "My Love for *Entourage*." "I probably would have been more nervous about that than the game."

The Badgers would need a second-half comeback to do it, but they ultimately took down North Carolina, 79-72, on Thursday and spent Friday night at the movies. The team signed waivers promising not to disclose details of the film before settling in alongside Ellin and Ferrara, who was also watching the completed movie for the first time. A backlot tour of the Warner Brothers studios wrapped up an unforgettable night.

"It was fun that the team got to do some of the Hollywood-type things when we were in L.A.," Bo Ryan remembered. "I was able to trust the guys that they wouldn't let it become a negative distraction. They were always able to separate when it was time to have fun and when it was time to work hard."

Pretty safe to assume teams at the other regional sites – Syracuse, Cleveland and Houston – didn't have this much fun. ∎

ARIZONA: THE SEQUEL

"We knew they were still upset and wanted revenge."

The Badgers were enjoying the quintessential L.A. experience. Five-star hotel, private movie screening at Warner Brothers, swapping digits with celebrities, names on the marquee at the Staples Center, their lives had been playing out like a movie script.

But one thing stood in the way of leaving Southern California with a Hollywood ending.

Almost a year to the date after Wisconsin squeaked out a 64-63 overtime win against Arizona in the Elite Eight, the Badgers and Wildcats were set to stage a rematch of one of the greatest games of the 2014 NCAA Tournament.

For the last 12 months Wisconsin had lived with the indigestion of its bitter loss to Kentucky in the Final Four. The Badgers had vowed to return to that spot and make amends.

For the Arizona Wildcats, the Badgers were Kentucky. Ever since their heart-stopping stumble in Anaheim, the Wildcats had targeted returning to the Elite Eight and, this time, getting over the hurdle.

They hadn't forgotten.

"I saw Rondae Hollis-Jefferson over the summer and he was like 'Don't talk to me. I don't mess with you,'" Sam Dekker chuckled. "He was obviously joking but it stuck with him. He was saying things like 'We'll get you next year.'"

"Every time I saw Sam Dekker, I would mention that game," Hollis-Jefferson added. "Even if it was a joking manner or whatever — he knew the sincerity of it. So for us to be back in this position again is like, 'Tie your shoes. Let's get ready, Sam. Let's play.'"

A year earlier Arizona was the top seed and Wisconsin was No. 2. This time the seeds were reversed, but that was one of the only differences. The Badgers and Wildcats each boasted 34-3 records, conference championships and rosters full of players destined for the NBA.

"We knew they would be motivated," Josh Gasser said. "We knew they were still upset at coming so close to the Final Four the year before and wanted revenge. But to be honest, we didn't think that would matter because we were just as motivated."

Everyone acknowledged the symmetry from a year before.

Just before taking the court in the Elite Eight rematch with Arizona, Bo Ryan reminded his team to "stay in the moment." *By Patrick Herb*

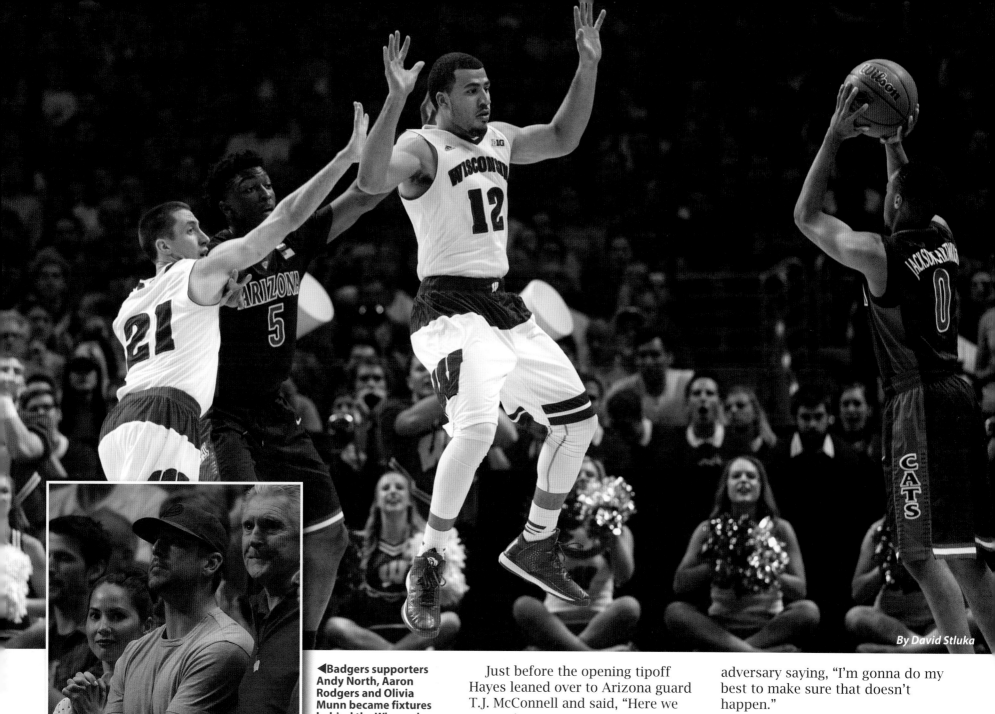

By David Stluka

◀ Badgers supporters Andy North, Aaron Rodgers and Olivia Munn became fixtures behind the Wisconsin bench in Los Angeles.
By Mark J. Terrill

Just before the opening tipoff Hayes leaned over to Arizona guard T.J. McConnell and said, "Here we are again, same spot, same time. Hopefully it ends the same way."

McConnell looked up at his adversary saying, "I'm gonna do my best to make sure that doesn't happen."

"Alright, you do that," Hayes replied.

More than McConnell, Arizona

Wisconsin singed the Staples Center nets with 10 second-half 3-pointers, shooting 79 percent from the field over the final 20 minutes (left to right: Gasser, Dekker, Kaminsky, Dukan). *By Icon Sportswire and David Stluka*

would need its big men to make sure a repeat didn't happen. A year earlier, Frank Kaminsky had torched the Wildcats for 28 points and 11 rebounds in the Badgers' win. This go-around, Arizona put forward Brandon Ashley and his 7-foot-3 wingspan on Kaminsky. The 2015 Pac-12 Tournament Most Outstanding Player, Ashley had missed the previous year's NCAA tournament with a foot injury. The defensive experiment wouldn't go well for the Cats.

On UW's first possession, Kaminsky finished off an and-one in the lane by drawing a foul on Ashley. Just 40 seconds later Ashley was headed to the bench with his second foul and UW's national player of the year had two more points from the free throw line.

Next up in the persecution post was Kaleb Tarczewski. This was not the 7-foot center's first introduction to Kaminsky, having drawn much of the defensive assignment the year before. In that game, Dekker was so caught up in his teammate's masterpiece that he couldn't resist innocently asking Tarczewski, "Isn't it tough to guard Frank?" Tarczewski replied, "I've never guarded someone like this. It's just awkward."

After his latest encounter with Kaminsky, Tarczewski may have used slightly different adjectives to describe checking the Badgers' superstar. Kaminsky would one-up his performance from a year earlier, leaving Arizona woozy with a game-high 29 points.

By halftime, all four of the Wildcats' post players were saddled with two fouls as Kaminsky and Dekker combined for 20 points in 20 minutes. But, identical to the prequel, Arizona still led by three at intermission.

Like UW, Arizona pounded the ball inside, resulting in 55 percent shooting as 28 of the Wildcats' 33 points came from the paint or the free throw line. They also put Kaminsky and Hayes on the bench late in the half with two fouls each.

"We knew it would be a fight, but we also felt that if we could just hit a few shots we would be alright," Bo Ryan said.

Right on cue, Kaminsky splashed a triple 13 seconds into the second half to tie the game. On the next possession Dekker drained a 3-pointer. By the time reserve Duje Dukan connected from long range two minutes later, Wisconsin had opened the half with a 14-3 run and surged to a 44-36 lead.

The Wildcats hung around, answering another Dekker 3 with back-to-back layups to get within 47-46 with 13:48 remaining. That was as close as Arizona would get.

"A team like that, you're not going to shut them out like 10 possessions in a row," Hayes, who had 15 points and seven offensive rebounds on the night, noted. "But

we did a good job of, if we scored, we weren't trading buckets. They were always in the game, but once we got on them, we did a great job of not letting them chip the lead away."

What unfolded next was a historic shooting display that sent the UW faithful into delirium and the Badgers back to the Final Four.

UW torched Arizona's No. 3-ranked defense with 10 second-half 3-pointers. The Badgers shot a dizzying 79 percent over the final 20 minutes, leaving Wildcats coach Sean Miller in disbelief.

"I mean, my god, there were so many 3s going in," he exasperated.

"I've never seen anything like that," Ryan marveled. "But that's the type of thing it takes to get to a Final Four. You have to have things fall in place."

Five different Badgers connected from downtown and every Wisconsin 3 seemed to build on the last. The Wildcats twice got within five points late, but both times it was Dekker throwing the dagger.

"When you're in the zone you don't have any worries," Dekker remembered of his career-high 27-point effort. "You just think everything you want to do will happen. That entire second half I felt like I could make plays to win the game. I just kind of caught fire with my jump shots and I rode it."

"That's the best I've ever seen him play, and I've been playing with him for years now, going back to AAU," Bronson Koenig gushed. "Just that second half was pretty crazy for him."

"Sam was unbelievable," Gasser added. "He came through when we needed it. He was the catalyst of it all. For him to show what he can do against one of the best defensive teams in the country and on the biggest stage possible, that was awesome. I was so happy for him."

Dekker's fourth 3 of the half pushed the Badgers ahead 79-71 with 1:51 remaining. But an Ashley three-point play with 51 seconds left gave the Cats some life, trailing 81-76.

Dekker time.

"We were trying to milk the clock and we knew they weren't going to foul," Dekker said. "We were going with a one-four down look with Bronson out high to take that shot. But he lost it in the middle of the play and I looked at the shot clock and it was only a couple seconds left so I had to run and get it. I saw a little alley down the sideline that I could get to and Rondae jumped and tried to block it, but I was able to push it up and kind of float it to the rim."

The next few seconds seemed like slow motion.

Dekker took two dribbles to his right and lofted a fadeaway rainmaker. From behind him on the bench Traevon Jackson stood and yelled "Buckets!" knowing it was pure. Ryan leaned, trying to will the ball through the cylinder. The capacity crowd held its breath as the ball took an eternity to come down.

SPLASH!

From his front row seat 10 feet away, Green Bay Packers quarterback Aaron Rodgers threw his hands in the air beaming with pride as he watched the heroics of his close friend.

Standing near midcourt, Gasser turned to TBS analyst Reggie Miller, a notoriously clutch shooter in his day, and mouthed the words, "Sam's got stones like you." Miller could only laugh and nod.

Dekker winked at Ryan, his coach patting him on the backside as he strutted down the sideline. "That was cold-blooded," Ryan would say after the game.

In all, the West Region Most Outstanding Player went 5-for-5 from 3-point range during his torrid second half, sending the crowd's emotions in opposite directions.

"Sam Dekker…" Arizona's McConnell stumbled through watery eyes after the game, "pretty much just crushed our dreams with that shot."

From his courtside table, voice of the Badgers Matt Lepay looked at the 85-78 final score and roared, "And it's over! The Wisconsin Badgers move on to Indianapolis… they will return to the Final Four!"

Dekker and Gasser embraced at midcourt as their teammates flooded onto the floor singing "Who's birthday is it?" one of thousands of quirky inside jokes that personified this Badgers team. NCAA president Mark Emmert handed the West Regional championship trophy to Wisconsin's four seniors and the party was on. Underneath black hats with the words "REGIONAL CHAMPIONS" stitched in gold, the Badgers checked another goal off their preseason wish list and celebrated like a team making back-to-back Final Fours for the first time in school history.

"It's hard to get back to a Final Four," Gasser said looking back. "The entire offseason you'd have people tell you, 'Oh you'll get back,' or 'Can't wait to see you in the Final Four again next year.' As players you're thinking, 'It's really tough. You don't just get back automatically.'

"Most players don't get to experience a Final Four and for those that do it's usually a once-in-a-lifetime moment. We were confident, but to actually do it and accomplish that was so gratifying."

Dekker's fifth and final 3-pointer, a rainbow over the out-stretched Rondae Hollis-Jefferson, evoked memories of his shot to win the high school state championship three years earlier. *By Icon Sportswire*

118

▲ "And it's over! The Wisconsin Badgers move on to Indianapolis… they will return to the Final Four!" – Voice of the Badgers Matt Lepay. *By Jae C. Hong*

By Patrick Herb

By David Stluka

"It's an incredible feeling," Kaminsky grinned.

Ryan hugged his wife, Kelly, and his grandkids, who had streamed onto the playing surface. Rodgers congratulated Dekker at midcourt with a high five and hug. Kaminsky threw on his GoPro camera, capturing every euphoric moment like the team hoisting Ryan onto their shoulders. "OK, put Pops down gently," Hayes joked.

The on-court feeling was elated déjà vu. But by the time the team returned to the locker room, the tenor was nothing like the year before.

"We celebrated making the Final Four this year, but it wasn't the party like it was in 2014," Gasser admitted. "The year before the feeling was like, 'We made it. This is as good as it gets.' This year when we got past Arizona there was a short celebration, but it was quickly on to the next goal. We were happy but we weren't satisfied in the least."

"The mindset was different because we almost expected to win at that point in the season," Kaminsky elaborated. "It didn't feel like win-or-go-home time, it was more of an expectation to win. We were excited and everything, but once that excitement was over we knew that we had a big task in front of us if we wanted to go further than the year before."

The year before the Badgers might not have even known – or cared – who they would play in the Final Four in Dallas. In 2015, everyone knew what was on the horizon.

"When we got into the locker room, we immediately were thinking about who is next," Gasser noted. "Kentucky and Notre Dame were playing after us and we were all sitting on our phones checking the score and following the game because there was no TV in the locker room. It was a very different focus this year."

So who were they rooting for, top-ranked and undefeated Kentucky or upset-minded Notre Dame?

"Honestly, I wanted to play Kentucky," Gasser allowed. "Usually you root for the underdog and want to play a lower seed, but that was one instance where I really wanted Kentucky to win. I wanted a shot at 38-0. You heard about Kentucky all year and they were this invincible team and they were unbeatable. But I knew we were just as good as them. You want to beat the best and you want a shot at them. Plus, revenge is sweet."

For now, the Badgers would leave L.A. savoring their fourth championship of the season. Thank you Hollywood and good night. ∎

THE LOCAL LEGEND

"Competing is the only way Dekker knows."

When Sam Dekker flicked his wrist and released a fadeaway rainbow from the right wing in the waning moments of Wisconsin's Elite Eight win over Arizona, Bo Ryan could have sworn he'd seen that play before.

Because he had.

Three years earlier, on the day Ryan's Badgers beat Vanderbilt in the 2012 NCAA Tournament, Ryan sat in the team hotel in Albuquerque, New Mexico, and watched a clip of his prized recruit. A thousand miles away, Dekker was writing one of the first chapters of his storied basketball career.

With 13.2 seconds remaining and his team down two in the Wisconsin High School State Championship, Dekker took the ball the length of the court and raised up for an off-balanced 3. Dekker's game-winner from the right wing – the identical spot from which he would sink Arizona – barely missed the outstretched defender's hand and hit nothing but net.

Déjà vu.

Dekker's dagger for Sheboygan Lutheran was a mainstay on ESPN's Play of the Week for over a month. The YouTube clip has been viewed well over a half-million times.

On that day in Madison in 2012, Dekker's legend was launched. In 2015 in Los Angeles, it was cemented.

"He hit that shot against Arizona and he turned and winked at me," Ryan said with a smile. "I just patted him on the back side. What are you gonna do?"

When the Sheboygan, Wisconsin, native arrived on campus in Madison in the summer of 2012, it seemed his career was destined for moments like that Staples Center clincher. Moments that would reduce Turner analyst Reggie Miller to simply laughing in wonderment. Moments that bring championships to the state of Wisconsin.

A top-20 recruit who committed to Ryan before his junior year of

A celebrity since high school, Dekker took his game to new heights during the 2015 NCAA Tournament, averaging more than 19 points per game and earning West Region Most Outstanding Player honors. **By Kendall Shaw | Cal Sport Media**

high school, Dekker had a rare combination of size, athleticism, skill and, as the wink indicated, moxie.

Ryan called offering a scholarship to the skinny 16-year old a "no-brainer," citing his feel for the game and the way he competed.

Competing is the only way Dekker knows. A coach's son and six years the junior of his brother, John, Sam was groomed competing against bigger, stronger kids. So when he arrived at UW, he was used to taking his licks and getting back up. But the transition wouldn't be easy for someone whose legend preceded him.

"He came in with unfairly high expectations," Gasser explained. "He played really well his first two years at Wisconsin but I think people expected him to score like 20 points per game or something. That just doesn't happen. But to break out in big games like he did in the NCAA tournament was important not only for his future, but for his legacy here at Wisconsin."

But before he could write that legacy, with games like his 23-point, 10-rebound effort against North Carolina or his 27-point virtuoso performance against Arizona that earned him 2015 West Region Most Outstanding Player honors,

Dekker had a lot of growing to do. In both senses of the word.

Over the span of three seasons, Dekker transformed into a player that could handle the rigors of the Big Ten. A player who was physically ready to swim in the NBA waters after three seasons at UW – a decision nobody questioned.

Dekker grew a full two inches, to 6-foot-9, and added roughly 35 pounds, exiting at a sturdy 230.

But his biggest growth might have come in the mental sense. Through his first two seasons on campus, during which he played in all 73 games and averaged more than 11.0 points per game, Dekker steadily learned what it took to succeed at a Big Ten level and become the all-around player he yearned to be.

But it was in the summer of 2014 that the humble, good-natured junior made the biggest leap. Dekker was invited to the prestigious Kevin Durant Skills Academy and had the chance to measure his game against the nation's top collegiate wing players. His performance gained him another invite, this time to the ultra-exclusive LeBron James Skills Academy in July. So impressive was Dekker that media, coaches and NBA

Since arriving in Madison, Dekker grew two inches and put on roughly 35 pounds. *By John Fisher | Cal Sport Media*

scouts came away almost unanimously picking him as the camp's standout player.

When James himself joined the action, he asked onlookers who he should guard, who is the best kid on the floor?

"He jumped in the game I was playing in and said, 'Alright, I got Dekks," Dekker remembered James saying. "Nobody ever calls me 'Dekks,' but that was pretty cool. I'm not going to say I dominated LeBron James or anything because I'm sure he wasn't going his hardest, but I think I held my own."

Already a self-confident kid, the experience sent Dekker back to Madison looking for more.

"The summer between my sophomore and junior seasons was huge confidence-wise," he said. "I matured a lot both mentally and physically. Playing in those camps with the best players in the country and with pros helped me realize how good I can be and that I hadn't tapped my full potential. It reminded me that I can play against big-time players. I brought that confidence home with me and worked even harder."

Strength and conditioning coach Erik Helland, who oversees the Badgers' summer workouts, agreed. But for Helland, the best part of Dekker's progression was how he steadily translated the summer success to

the season.

"Sam had an outstanding summer, but what was one of the most gratifying things was that it didn't automatically flip a switch that made him a completely different person," Helland observed. "He had better tools at that point, but as you saw him through the season, you saw an offensively-talented player become a balanced basketball player. He became a better defender, a better rebounder, a better facilitator of others, a better ability to take contact. What you saw was that gradual process of him integrating

some of these new abilities to become a complete player.

"As the season progresses, the competition gets tougher, the stage gets bigger. Do players have the capacity to grow, adapt, find a way to overcome failures and cope with new challenges? The growth that Sam, and others, showed was remarkable and rewarding to witness."

That completeness came full circle in the 2015 national semifinal against Kentucky. Dekker will be remembered for his gigantic step-back 3-pointer that broke a 60-60 tie with under 2:00 remaining, but it was a play 20 seconds later, at the other end of the floor, that made his head coach proud.

Dekker would cut off a driving Trey Lyles and take a violent charge in the lane, providing a pivotal stop and returning the basketball to Wisconsin.

"I think of all the things I ever did, that one probably surprised Coach the most," Dekker chuckled, recalling one of the four charges he took in his career.

"He made a play and he did what it took to win," Ryan said, giving about as big a compliment as he can give. "From the time Sam came into the program we were always trying to get him to understand that you're never finished. If you score or make a play, you gotta get back on defense, you gotta help and recover, you gotta block out. There is always something else to do. Sam learned that over his three-year career. He learned to become more focused, more consistent and take care of the little things."

"That's gratifying to see," Ryan added proudly. "And it put us in the championship game."

As the Badgers navigated one of the toughest NCAA tournament gauntlets you'll find, Dekker seemed to relish the big stage as much as anyone.

"Toward the end of the season I started to look forward to big games," Dekker admitted. "All the perseverance was worth it. It was the best time of year to make an impact."

No one was happier about Dekker's emergence than his teammates. A guy that is almost never in a bad mood with an endearingly silly sense of humor, Dekker deserved this success.

"I was really happy for Sam the way he played late in the season," Josh Gasser said. "He needed that. After the Big Ten tournament championship game he was happy that we won, but he was a little down

because he didn't play that well. He wanted to experience us winning with him playing well."

"It was fun to watch Sam's confidence and game explode in the NCAA tournament," Kaminsky agreed. "We all knew he had it in him and he picked a perfect time to bring it out."

On April 10, Dekker penned a letter to Wisconsin fans signifying the end of his time in the Cardinal and White. Declaring for the 2015 NBA Draft after three seasons in Madison, the local-kid-made-good put a bow on a career that featured more than 1,000 points and equally as many memories.

To the Badger Nation,

I really don't know where to start. Most importantly, I just want to say thank you.

These past three years have been the best, most memorable years of my life. Growing up in the state and being able to wear Wisconsin across my chest has been a dream come true.

It has been a true honor to represent this University and the state of Wisconsin. I can't say enough about how much all of your support has meant to me and my teammates. The privilege of playing in front of a sold out Kohl Center or looking around at the sea of red that filled Lucas Oil Stadium last weekend are things that most college basketball players never get to experience and I never took that for granted. Badgers fans are the greatest in the world.

After lots of thoughts and prayers, I've decided that it is in my best interest to enter the NBA Draft at this time. It is difficult to leave Madison and the only state I've called home, but I'm excited for the next chapter of my life.

I truly can't say thank you enough to my teammates, coaches, training staff and you, the fans, for everything you've done. I am so grateful for the opportunities Coach Ryan and UW–Madison have given me. I couldn't have asked for anything more from my experience.

I will continue to represent the University and entire state of Wisconsin to the best of my ability wherever my future takes me. I will never forget these years as a Badger; not just for the basketball victories, but for the friends made, lessons learned and the memories that will last a lifetime.

God Bless and On Wisconsin!

Sam

THE PROMISED LAND ISN'T PROMISED...
it's earned

Traveon Jackson was jolted awake as he felt the airplane wheels connect with the runaway. As he slid the West Regional Champions cap away from his face, he peeked out the window at the dark and sleepy Madison airport. It was after 3 a.m. and the only welcome committee awaiting a Badgers team that had just secured back-to-back Final Four appearances was an idling bus and a few weary-looking members of the airport ground crew.

This was a far cry from the scene one year earlier when the Badgers had taken a victory cruise to the Kohl Center accompanied by the wailing sirens of Madison Fire Department trucks. In 2014, after a scintillating win over Arizona, Wisconsin returned the following afternoon and was greeted by more than 10,000 delirious fans for a welcome home pep rally.

"The days between the Elite Eight and the Final Four that first year were crazy," Duje Dukan explained. "It was a huge party at the Kohl Center that day we got back and everywhere we went people recognized you as a basketball player – even guys that didn't play a lot. People would stop you, say 'Congratulations, you guys are on an unbelievable ride, keep it up.'"

"There was such a feeling of 'we made it' that first year," Frank Kaminsky added. "You couldn't help kind of getting swept up in it."

When the players left the Kohl Center rally they were still wearing their Final Four shirts and hats, relishing in the accomplishment and proud to show off their reward. Kaminsky and Josh Gasser couldn't even make the three-block walk to Chipotle for dinner.

"People were going crazy and you couldn't walk 10 feet without somebody wanting to congratulate you or take a picture or get an autograph," Kaminsky remembered. "You literally couldn't go anywhere without being patted on the back."

In 2015, they would have no such trouble.

"When we came back to Madison after reaching the second Final Four, it was late at night and all of the students were on spring break," Gasser said. "We would walk around campus that week and almost no one said a word to us because no one was around.

"It was almost like you didn't accomplish anything yet. There was no one patting you on the back yet. I liked that a lot because we all knew we had more to do."

"I think it was good for us that we got home in the middle of night," Sam Dekker agreed. "I know people celebrated back in Madison after we beat Arizona, but by the time we got home everything was quiet. We weren't satisfied just getting to the Final Four. That was only a step in reaching our goal of the national championship. Maybe it was good that we didn't let ourselves feel satisfied."

Or as Kaminsky put it, "We knew there was a lot left to be done."

◆◆◆◆

Things were different when the team landed in Indianapolis as well. A Wisconsin custom-decaled Indy car led the Badgers' processional from the airport, Final Four logos adorned nearly every flat surface of downtown and the towering Lucas Oil Stadium was lit up just two blocks from UW's team hotel. But there was a calmness, a poise that replaced the giddy amazement a year earlier.

"We weren't in awe at everything this time around," Dekker conceded. "The first Final Four was a stepping stone for this program and it was almost surreal to us that we were there and walking into the football stadium and thinking how cool it was. This year we were more focused on knowing what it's like and being prepared. The gym didn't seem as big, the media didn't seem as huge and the lights didn't seem so bright. We felt very calm about it. We expected to be there and we deserved to be there. Having the previous experience prepared us for this run."

As the players went from camera to camera and station to station fulfilling three hours of media obligations two days prior to the game, the attitude was different as well. It was subtle – they still wore ridiculous

Sam Dekker and Nigel Hayes couldn't resist the photo-op in the custom-painted Indy cars when the Badgers arrived at the Final Four.
By Brandon Harrison

costumes, mugged for lenses and enjoyed the moment – but the silliness was tempered. The Badgers didn't dance quite as hard on the TV production set that would make a Hollywood movie blush; a voiceover that might have taken four takes a year ago was taking just two this go-around.

"The biggest difference was, we had been there so we kind of understood the hoopla and all the media attention and fans," Gasser noted. "But more importantly, I think we expected to win the whole thing. We were happy to be there but we weren't satisfied at all."

They had also been preparing for this weekend for a long time.

"I talked about that with so many people," Kaminsky offered. "The minute the

tournament bracket came out and I saw our path, I said it's going to be the exact same thing as last year. We're going to beat Arizona and return to the exact same spot, the same stage, except this time we're going to beat Kentucky. It was destiny."

In truth, the footing for Wisconsin's rematch with Kentucky in the Final Four was laid long before Selection Sunday.

The Badgers didn't need reminding.

Exactly 364 days had passed since Aaron Harrison's devastating 3-pointer at AT&T Stadium in Texas. Exactly zero days had passed without thoughts of that shot.

That shot, that game, had reduced the

Wisconsin locker room to tears and anger. It also served as Day One of the Badgers' year-long mission to return to this crossroads.

Gasser tried to not think about it but would have flashbacks at the most random moments. Dekker had changed his Twitter header to a photo of Kentucky's on-court celebration as a daily reminder. Kaminsky wrote a blog about it saying, "I am positive I will never watch that Kentucky game from start to finish because I hate seeing myself losing."

No, the Badgers didn't need reminding. But there it was. In a ballroom at the Omni Hotel in Indianapolis, the Wisconsin players sat restlessly as the video whirred during the team's scouting report. They were watching cut-ups of Kentucky's personnel. Highlights

By Brandon Harrison

were largely from the season, but of course contained possessions from the previous year's meeting.

Towards the end of the scouting report, there it was. Harrison lifting up from five feet outside the 3-point arc, firing over an out-stretched Gasser from the left wing.

A team that could hardly turn down the volume on their never-ending playful chatter was reduced to mute. Just outside the door, Badgers fans were reveling in the hotel lobby, but inside the team room: blackout. Nothing needed to be said.

"It got really silent and almost awkward," Gasser remembered. "The coaches didn't even say anything about the clip and they always have something to say, telling us what we should have done differently or how to handle something.

"I remember hoping the Harrison shot wouldn't be in our clips and thinking that the coaches probably wouldn't include it. But after seeing it and feeling that room, I was glad it was in there."

Minutes after that fateful 2014 loss, Kaminsky sat in the emotionally destroyed locker room and vowed to reporters, "We are going to be back next year. We are going to be better than ever. We will all be ready. It is going to be a long road to get back to here, but I know we will make it."

They did make it. Now, as the Badgers sat in their quiet cocoon of a film room, they knew they were just one day away from the rarest of opportunities. Life doesn't typically offer second chances, do-overs, but the Badgers were now on the threshold of redemption.

Publicly, the team would say they didn't care who they were playing, it was just another step to a larger goal. Privately, they wanted – they needed – to play Kentucky.

◆◆◆◆

Taking the court for the Final Four had a familiarity for Wisconsin. They had made that long run from the locker room to the court before, they had shot against a cavernous football stadium backdrop, they had stood toe-to-toe with Kentucky just a year ago. But there was one thing that was unfamiliar.

Wisconsin would enter the national semifinal as a heavy underdog. The Badgers had been David to Goliath just one other time that entire season, and that was by the slimmest of margins one game earlier against Arizona. This time, Las Vegas had Kentucky six points better than the Badgers. And the Wildcats had earned that line.

The entire 2014-15 season felt like a victory lap for Kentucky. Big Blue Nation took up residence atop the polls in Week One and never relinquished the spot, running roughshod through the season. There was the 32-point shellacking of No. 5 Kansas on November 18 or the 18-2 run to open the second half and run away from No. 6 Texas on December 5. Then came December 20 in Chicago when Kentucky embarrassed UCLA, scoring the game's first 24 points before letting off the gas and "only" winning by 39.

"When somebody asked me about Kentucky being ranked number one during the season, I made the joke that Kentucky Blue is number one and Kentucky White should be number two. They were that dominant," Bo Ryan said of the Wildcats platoon playing rotation that exchanged fivesomes of high school All-Americans.

Kentucky had a few scares on the way – like back-to-back overtime wins in the SEC – but those only seemed to strengthen its resolve and lend credence to the mantra that this was a team of destiny. The Wildcats ripped through the SEC tournament and opening games of the Big Dance without breaking a sweat. Long before UK pulverized

West Virginia, 78-39, in the Sweet 16, the Wildcats vs. the NCAA tournament field was an even bet in Las Vegas.

An exasperated Mountaineers coach Bob Huggins left Quicken Loans Arena saying, "That's the best defensive team I think I've ever coached against. And when they're making shots, there's nobody going to best them." UCLA's Steve Alford said the same thing in December.

The question was never if the Wildcats would win, but in what obnoxious fashion. The Wildcats were never battling this year's crop of opponents, they were battling history. This felt like Tiger Woods chasing Jack Nicklaus' majors record. This was Hank Aaron swinging for Babe Ruth's home run crown.

The Wall Street Journal ran a story about Kentucky in November that began with the question, "Are they not just the best college basketball team now... but maybe ever?"

In the Elite Eight, Kentucky outlasted a talented Notre Dame squad, rubber stamping the formality of reaching the Final Four. With a roster loaded with future NBA players, UK was the first team in 24 years to enter the final weekend without a loss and the first team ever to start a season 38-0.

Kentucky was better than it was in 2014. But so was Wisconsin.

As Duke was putting the finishing touches on a win over Michigan State in the first game of the Final Four doubleheader, deep in the recesses of Lucas Oil Stadium, Bo Ryan paced in front of his team. Seated neatly in three rows, 16 pairs of eyes tracked their leader as he wore out a stretch of carpet in the front of the locker room.

"You've got to remember to block out. You can't let them kill you on the glass. They're going to try to drive into you. You

From the pregame speech to the pregame introductions, anticipation for Wisconsin vs. Kentucky was at a fevered pitch. ▲By Patrick Herb ▼By David J. Phillip

need to move your feet. You've got to chest them up."

Ryan was reciting the same keys he had highlighted all week in practice. The same tenets of Wisconsin basketball that helped him win more games than any coach in school history. As he called the players to their feet, he gathered them in close. The team with an unrivaled brotherhood was standing tight enough to nearly feel each other's heartbeat. Ryan waited a moment before he delivered one final truth.

"Gentlemen," Ryan began slowly. "The Promised Land isn't promised... it's earned. Now go get it."

Like a heavyweight fight after a series of undercards, Wisconsin vs. Kentucky was the main event Saturday night in Indianapolis. Duke had yawned past Michigan State, 81-61, in the earlier bout. The highlight of the opening contest even came before the tipoff when Badgers sophomore Vitto Brown – dressed in full game uniform – joined a student-athlete from Duke, MSU and UK to sing the national anthem.

By the time the Badgers and Wildcats took the floor it was after 9 p.m. and the crowd of 72,238 was worked into an anxious lather. Big Blue Nation outnumbered Badger Nation by a noticeable margin, but that only seemed to strengthen the vocal chords of Wisconsin fans. And as the game unfolded, the team in red would gain supporters by the minute.

For an atmosphere that is often filled with corporate or neutral on-lookers, the marquee matchup had the feeling of a crosstown high school rivalry.

"Looking around Lucas Oil Stadium at all the red was unbelievable," Ryan beamed. "I don't usually notice the crowd or the atmosphere, but sometimes you have to look around and file things away for memories. Every time I've been to a Final Four that Kentucky was playing in, they have always had the loudest introductions. I listened to the sound in Indy – we matched that, and then some."

Big Ten Network's Dave Revsine would tweet pregame, "Not sure I can recall a Final 4 where there was this much emotion in building - as good an atmosphere as u can get for hoops in a FB stadium."

The game would not disappoint.

Kentucky opened with a 3-pointer and breakaway alley-oop, but Wisconsin answered right back. By the time the

teams retreated to their corners at the first media timeout the score read 9-9 and both sets of fans – red and blue – were standing and applauding. What more could you want?

"It was a great environment," Gasser said, thinking back. "Big Blue Nation is ruthless, they show up, they scream and they have a great team to support. Just walking on the court you see how big those Kentucky guys are; we can't emulate that in practice at all. It was a little shocking at first, but we settled in quickly."

Alternating 3-pointers and attacking the rim, the Badgers pushed out to a nine-point lead midway through the first half, the Wildcats' largest deficit of the tournament. After powering through UK's Devin Booker in the post for a three-point play, Dekker pointed to his biceps, signifying that on this night the Badgers would be the ones doing the pushing around.

Through 15 minutes, Wisconsin had controlled the pace, and equally as important, the rebounds. The Badgers had five offensive rebounds to Kentucky's zero, despite UK's daunting frontline of Willie Cauley-Stein, Karl-Anthony Towns, Dakari Johnson, Trey Lyles and Marcus Lee — who stood 7-0, 7-0, 6-11, 6-10 and 6-9.

"If you're going into a game scared, you're not going to win," Dekker said. "It didn't matter to us who we were playing. We didn't look at them as too big or too physical. Kentucky was a good team, but we were ready for it. As talented as they were, so were we and we really believed we had a better team."

A Lyles breakaway tomahawk dunk gave the Cats a 36-34 lead with 31 seconds left in the half but Bronson Koenig's deep jumper just before the buzzer tied the game at

intermission. Just as it appeared destined to be.

Take a bow, basketball Gods.

"I have a feeling this was one of those games that when the replay airs as one of those 'Instant Classics,' it will get a pretty good rating," Ryan grinned of the contest that was watched by 22.6 million people, garnering the highest Final Four rating in 22 years.

One of countless storylines that had people clamoring for Wisconsin vs. Kentucky to be a seven-game series was the clash of historically good offense vs. once-in-a-generation defense. The Badgers led the nation in adjusted offensive efficiency that season, with a sizzling average of 127.9 points per 100 possessions – the highest number since famed statistician Ken Pomeroy began tracking it in 2002. Across the court, Kentucky entered the game with the lowest adjusted defensive efficiency number (86.1 points per 100 possessions) in the history of Pomeroy's database. The classic paradox: unstoppable force meets immovable object.

As the second half began it appeared elite offense would get the better of top-ranked defense. UW scored 16 points on its first eight possessions as consecutive three-point plays from Kaminsky and Dekker and a long-range hit from Koenig pushed UW ahead 52-44. Kentucky entered the game allowing just 53.9 points per game. The Badgers would reach that with 11:30 remaining.

Through three quarters, Wisconsin had managed to keep its head above water. But the big blue tide kept rising. The Badgers' eight-point lead began to shrivel.

With 5:16 left to play, Wisconsin had every reason to come unraveled.

The lead the Badgers had enjoyed all half was gone. Kentucky had surged ahead 60-56 and the roar from Big Blue Nation was almost deafening. The Wildcats' headliner defense

was squeezing the life out of the Badgers, holding UW without a field goal for more than seven minutes. For a brief stretch, it even appeared the team in red was battling the stripes, watching three questionable officiating calls go the wrong way.

First a Gasser charge negated a Koenig 3-pointer; then an open-handed blow from Trey Lyles to the chin of Gasser was reviewed and ruled no foul, despite all three CBS announcers conceding it was, at a minimum, a Flagrant 1 offense; finally a Nigel Hayes push-off on the ensuing possession nearly sent Ryan into hysteria.

The Badgers appeared dangerously close to becoming an afterthought in Kentucky's pursuit of perfection.

"There are times in my coaching career where I might have thought, 'uh oh,' or sensed that we were tired," Ryan said. "But with this group and what we had been through, I knew they weren't going to let something like this discourage them."

Showing the resolve of a veteran team that had won 65 games over the last two years, the Badgers would take a punch (literally as it were) and get back up. UW started by forcing a shot clock violation. Then Dekker swooped down the lane and finished a finger roll in traffic to cut the deficit to two. Another defensive shot clock violation put the ball back in the hands of the Badgers as the game reached the final media timeout.

"People might have thought trailing with three minutes left would be a time to get tight, but in the huddle we had the opposite thought, that there were still three long minutes to go," Kaminsky offered. "We knew if we made a couple plays we would win the game. I think everybody on our team believed we were going to win before the game even started. If you think about it, it's almost destiny in a way. We were in a similar situation last year and we didn't respond well. So we went back to school, figured everything out and then returned to the same situation and we almost knew exactly what was going to happen."

"Even in that final timeout, in that situation, they were themselves," Ryan added. "I didn't see any panic, any anxiety. That's what experience can do for you. I told them, 'We're right where we always wanted to be. All that talk, all that work, we're right where we need to be.'"

With just over 2:30 remaining, Hayes rebounded his own miss and scored the game-tying basket just as the shot clock expired. Kentucky players tried to wave it off and coach John Calipari pleaded for a shot-clock violation, but such a play was not reviewable until the final two minutes of the game. Tie game, 60-60.

"Before or after the shot clock, whichever one you want to say," Gasser said of the controversial play, "that was a big turning point. I think it kind of shook them up a little bit, so that was a big play."

The Badgers' defense had ratcheted up – shutting out UK on five consecutive possessions – and so had its offense. Another Cats miss late in the shot clock gave UW the ball back at the two-minute warning.

"Kentucky went on their run, but then we knew it was our time," Dekker said. "Frank carried us, but we had a bunch of different guys stepping up late in that game. That was good to see, how much we were all on board for a common purpose. We didn't worry, we didn't waver. That's how we were all season and that's the sign of a well-coached team."

Dekker was one of those guys stepping up late. Just like he did the weekend before against Arizona, he seemed to relish the big moment, burying a silky step-back 3-pointer from the top of the arc. The rainbow shot gave the Badgers a three-point lead and had CBS' Bill Raftery shouting, "Early ONIONS! Wow!"

"We called something where Frank could come and ball screen for me and that's something that has been working for us as of late," Dekker, who finished with 16 points, said after the game. "(Towns) came off it and got on his heels a little bit. He thought I was going to drive and I was able to free up some space on a step-back. I was waiting for a good look like that all night. As soon as it was off my hand I knew it was down."

A mere 17 seconds later, Dekker was making another big play, absorbing a charge from UK's Lyles that sent him

"Even in that final timeout, in that situation, they were themselves. I didn't see any panic, any anxiety. That's what experience can do for you." - Bo Ryan *By Michael Conroy*

sprawling to the floor and had Ryan punching the air with a two-handed fist pump. Dekker would add a free throw, but a three-point play from Wildcats guard Aaron Harrison pulled UK within 64-63 with 56 seconds on the clock.

Desperately needing a bucket to keep Goliath at arm's length, Wisconsin went to its bread winner. Kaminsky, who finished with a game-high 20 points and 11 rebounds, drew a foul on Cauley-Stein with a drop step spin move worthy of his player of the year portfolio. Kaminsky hit both free throws, but a foul at the other end gave the Wildcats a point back.

UW's lead was two, 66-64, with 12.2 seconds remaining as a quick Kentucky foul sent Koenig to the line. The same player who had knocked down two knee-knockers in the closing seconds of regulation in the Big Ten

tournament championship game was faced with a pair of throws that could all but seal it for Wisconsin.

As he took the long walk down the court, Koenig felt Hayes sidle up next to him and say, "Take us home. They don't call you 'Clutch B' for nothing!"

As Koenig toed the free throw line atop the elevated court, it fittingly resembled a stage. Live theater at its best.

Swish. Swish.

When an Aaron Harrison deep 3 found nothing but air, the Wisconsin celebration had begun. The scar tissue from a year ago began to loosen. A collection of veterans and talent who had matured at different speeds, the Badgers rose with the pressure. The difference between being microwaved and a slow marinade.

Hayes jumped up and down like he was on

Dekker's step-back 3-pointer and charge on the ensuing possession gave the Badgers the lead – and momentum – they would never relinquish." *By Icon Sportswire*

a pogo stick and Kaminsky pumped his fist and released a primal yell. Dekker skipped down the court urging the crowd to its feet. He may not have realized they had been standing for nearly the entire second half. If they could have levitated, they surely would have.

"What an awesome feeling," Gasser beamed. "To get the rematch with Kentucky, the number one team, 38-0, all that stuff, and win was just incredible. We truly believed we were going to win. Not that we had a chance, but that we were the better team. We played

our hearts out and proved that we were the better team on that night, and that's all that matters."

As the final buzzer sounded, the Wisconsin bench poured onto the floor looking for anyone to hug and jumping on each other's backs. Amidst "On, Wisconsin!" from the Badger band and chants of "Thiry-eight and done!" from the UW student section, Kaminsky stomped around the court displaying a shirt emblazoned with the team's season-long mantra: "Make 'Em Believe."

The Badgers had slayed the dragon and officially made believers of a nation. Final score: Wisconsin 71, Kentucky 64.

Wisconsin had advanced to the national championship after blistering Kentucky's stonewall defense with an average of 1.23

132

points per possession and dominating the Wildcats by an almost unthinkable 34-22 rebounding margin.

One year earlier, the Badgers and Wildcats had produced one of the great games in recent Final Four memory. They somehow topped it in 2015.

"We've all been around either as a fan or as a player or as a broadcaster. This was one of the great, classic semifinal games we have all ever seen," CBS's Jim Nantz would say as he signed off the broadcast.

As "Jump Around" wailed through the speakers suspended above the stage, Lucas Oil Stadium morphed into Camp Randall. Kentucky's despondent fans couldn't reach the exits fast enough but no one wearing red was ready to leave. And why would they? Wisconsin basketball had the spotlight to itself and was going to soak up every ounce of shine.

The spontaneous party at the stadium was only rivaled by the one awaiting the Badgers an hour later at their team hotel.

"It was after one o'clock in the morning and I was expecting to grab some food, shower and go to sleep. I was exhausted and we had a big game coming up," Gasser said. "Little did I know we'd have thousands of Badgers fans in the streets, outside our hotel and in our lobby just screaming, partying and enjoying it. That was awesome."

The words fire code didn't apply. Badgers revelers had the Omni Hotel bursting at the seams as security tried desperately to rope off a path for the team to navigate the crowded streets and throng inside.

"That was ridiculous," Dekker said. "We were like 'Oh my goodness.' It was crazy, that's all you can really say about it. It was a crazy scene and it made you grateful for the support. I saw what it was like back in Madison and everyone was ridiculously excited there too. Badger Nation was out in full force."

The Badgers on-court celebration after beating Kentucky was only rivaled by the party awaiting them at their team hotel. Jordan Smith's selfie from the mezzanine illustrates the packed lobby at the Omni Hotel. *By Patrick Herb*

Wisconsin's postgame meal was waiting in a mezzanine-level hallway that was open to the lobby below. As the players appeared on the balcony, they took a moment to savor the spectacle. Hailed like they were the Beatles, the Badgers filmed the sea of red with their phones as the crowd below filmed them right back.

"The scene was crazy," Kaminsky added. "It was almost like the place to be in Indianapolis. Everyone down in the lobby just screaming every time they saw us. We kind of messed with the crowd a little bit. We all walked into the meal room and then walked back out to see how loud we could make it."

Kaminsky, who had celebrated his 22nd birthday with the win over Kentucky, was serenaded by the sea of red below. "I had 'Happy Birthday' sung to me more that day than I had in my entire life combined. Best birthday present ever."

From the top of the hotel lobby, they may as well have been on top of the world.

"That's one thing I'll never forget," Gasser said. "I have a picture of it in my phone that I'll probably save forever. It was crazy and it really shows how great our fans are. Sometimes you can take it for granted a little bit to play in front of a sold-out crowd every single night and always have fans travel for you, but that right there showed how great our fans are, how loyal they are and how great it is to be a Wisconsin Badger." ∎

THE ARCHITECT

"To be a Badger is great. To be a successful Badger is even better."

When Bo Ryan decides to do something, he does it all the way. Such was the case in the 1950s Biddy League championship game when he scored 40 points against a team coached by his father, Butch Ryan. Or the time in the late '70s when Ryan ran a half marathon, in basketball shoes, without training, just because he was challenged.

It was that way in 1984 when he stepped onto the campus of University of Wisconsin-Platteville and turned a dormant Division III basketball program into the winningest team in any division during the 1990s.

So in 2001, when William Francis Ryan was named the 15th head coach in Wisconsin history, why should anyone have expected anything different?

Despite getting the job at the tender age of 54, Ryan assured fans and media in his opening press conference that energy would never be a problem. In his 2008 biography *Another Hill to Climb*, he wrote about what he told those in attendance that first day on the job.

We can sell. We have a lot to sell. To be a Badger is great. To be a successful Badger is even better. This isn't an ending, this is a beginning.

He was right.

Bo Ryan's 14 seasons in Madison have produced seven Big Ten championships, 14 NCAA tournament appearances and now two Final Fours. **By David Stluka**

In 14 years in Madison, Ryan has taken a program just beginning to wake from a 50-year slumber and guided it into the pantheon of elite college basketball programs. He started by producing Big Ten regular season championships in each of his first two seasons at UW, something not seen in Madison since 1923 and 1924. Next came a Big Ten tournament championship in year three and an Elite Eight appearance in year

how good Coach Ryan is, but from a national perspective, I don't think Wisconsin and Coach Ryan have gotten the respect they deserve, to say the least," Josh Gasser added. "Reaching the first Final Four changed Coach Ryan's resume and then I think making the second Final Four kind of changed the status of the program into one of the elite."

"Coach Ryan's legacy speaks for itself," Frank Kaminsky offered. "The way he's built this program and taken it to an elite, national level is pretty crazy. The Dukes, North Carolinas and Kentuckys will always be on top of college basketball, but Wisconsin was never in that argument before. I think after the last two years we are now talked about as a national powerhouse. That's so crazy to think about that we changed the culture and Coach Ryan was at the helm of all that. I think his legacy definitely speaks for itself."

If you were to ask Ryan about his legacy, he'd probably say he's most proud of developing the men as much as cultivating the wins. It begins with the characteristics he looks for in his players.

"Good students, hard workers, good

four. By 2013 he had rewritten the school's wins record, taken UW to the NCAA tournament all 12 seasons and produced the best Big Ten winning percentage in conference history.

Stacking that on top of his four national championships and .822 career winning percentage at UW-Platteville, there wasn't much missing from his Hall of Fame resumé.

Then came 2014 and 2015 – back-to-back trips to the Final Four, college basketball's Holy Grail.

"The last two years have shown to the world of basketball what those who paid attention to Bo Ryan throughout his Wisconsin career understood immediately," stated Mike DeCourcy, longtime *Sporting News* columnist and member of the US Basketball Writers Association Hall of Fame. "Hiring Bo Ryan at Wisconsin is one of the greatest basketball hires in history. Wisconsin basketball was a program that could do good things in the right circumstance, but since Bo's been there it has been a consistent national power."

"People in Wisconsin have always known

listeners," Ryan said of the recruits he targets. "People that are pretty focused on what's going to happen in the next 60 years as much as they are focused on what's going to happen in the next couple years, because that's what we're preparing people for as coaches. We're preparing them for when they're in their 30s, 40s, 50s, 60s, 70s and 80s."

A former teacher, Ryan prides himself on coaching life lessons through the game of basketball. His players know it. His players appreciate it.

"I remember standing in the locker room while I was being recruited and listening to Coach Ryan talk to the team after a loss," Sam Dekker recalled. "He told them that every day you wake up with a blank canvas and you can paint it however you want. He said you need to go to bed at night and be able to look back and be proud of the picture you painted that day and then go out and improve on the painting the next day. I was in high school when I heard that and I still remember it like it was yesterday. It has stuck with me. Coach Ryan is a life coach as much as a basketball coach."

The caliber of men that exit the Wisconsin program speaks to the life coach. The student-athlete growth and wins speak to the basketball coach.

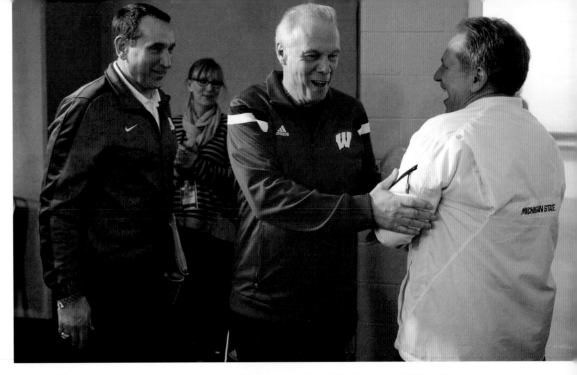

Perhaps the most star-studded Final Four in history, coaches Mike Krzyzewski, Tom Izzo, John Calipari and Bo Ryan own a combined 2,846 career wins. *By David J. Phillip*

"The player development you saw in taking Kaminsky from two points per game to player of the year, or Sam's progression or Nigel's improvement, speaks to what he has done for years," ESPN broadcaster Mike Tirico said. "With lesser skilled athletes at smaller levels, he maximized talent and won titles. These last two years have let everyone know that Bo Ryan is one of the best coaches ever."

"Coach Ryan's greatest strength is being able to read situations and knowing what has to be done," said Kaminsky, one of the greatest success stories in the history of college basketball. "It's not always the popular decision amongst players, but then again at the end of the day, it doesn't matter because it's his team and he knows what's best. Just being able to know what is needed and going out there and doing it on a day-to-day basis is something he's very good at."

Another thing his players have always appreciated is the flexibility he gives them. Mislabeled as rigid because of their methodical offensive approach and old-school attention to detail, the Badgers are anything but inelastic.

"He prepares us, then lets us play," Gasser explained. "We'd play some teams where the coach is screaming out

plays from the sidelines or yelling, 'Pull it out, pull it out.' Coach Ryan has never called a play during live action. But even during timeouts, he'll usually ask the guards what they want to run and we'll call a play. Throughout the whole flow of the game we control it. People don't think he lets us play but that's exactly what he does."

"It's a basic game and I love how the team coaches itself," legendary announcer Bill Raftery said of Ryan's team during the 2014-15 season. "By that, I mean Bo has taught them how to read situations and respond. You take what he has done here and his evolution as a coach towards the talent he

has, it proves the flexibility that he has in how he analyzes the game."

Ryan lives by mantras like "Scold to mold; praise to raise." But as 2015 proved, he's also the fun-loving coach that gives his team room to breathe.

"The attitude and the behavior that your coach displays will rub off on the team," Nigel Hayes said. "So if you have an uptight coach it kind of reflects in the team being uptight or stiff. They might play with the fear of making their coach mad. If the coach has an attitude that is complimentary of the team, it makes you more relaxed and, if you can play that way, the better you'll be. We

have that with Coach Ryan."

"Bo Ryan coaches them hard, but they never showed it," Tirico said. "The fact that Bo let them be who they are, yet gave them the great foundation, discipline and tenets, is why this worked so well."

The author of more than 700 wins, 18 conference championships and countless coach of the year accolades, Ryan's career is among the most decorated you'll find. Already a member of five halls of fame and counting, Ryan was one of 12 finalists for the Naismith Memorial Basketball Hall of Fame Class of 2015.

The inductees were announced during Final Four weekend in Indianapolis. Ryan's name wasn't called for the most prestigious honor in basketball, but it will be soon.

"These two years showed that Bo Ryan is a Hall of Fame coach," DeCourcy furthered. "I'm not sure people would have known that without this run. They should have, but sometimes people need that final bit of evidence. He did not make the Hall of Fame this time around, but with what has happened, I'm pretty sure he'll be there eventually."

"One of the biggest disappointments of Final Four weekend and biggest crimes was Bo not getting in the Hall of Fame," Tirico objected. "These last two years have certainly put Bo Ryan in a spotlight for everyone to see what a good coach he is. Given all he's accomplished, if that's not a Hall of Fame coach, I don't know what is." ■

"Coach Ryan's greatest strength is being able to read situations and knowing what has to be done. He knows what's best." – Frank Kaminsky *By David Stluka*

SO CLOSE, SO PROUD

"Thanks for taking us all on this ride."

A mere 18 hours after pulling off arguably the biggest win in school history, Bo Ryan settled into the front seat of the Wisconsin team bus. The Badgers had just completed the final practice of the season and now sat one day away from the ultimate prize.

As he watched the Lucas Oil Stadium façade shrink out his window, Ryan saw his phone light up on the open seat next to him. He almost didn't answer it. The phone had been buzzing non-stop since UW's 71-64 thriller over Kentucky.

He would be glad he took this call. On the other end of the line, North Carolina coach Roy Williams was making good on a promise he never got the chance to fulfill a year earlier.

When the two head coaches crossed paths in the summer of 2014, Williams told Ryan a story, "Bo, I was really pulling for you guys to make the championship game. If you would have, I was going to leave the seat next to me open. When anyone asked who was sitting there, I was going to tell them that it was saved for your dad, Butch. I'm sorry I never got that chance."

As everyone knows, the Badgers came one point short of reaching that 2014 Final Four. So when Ryan's team advanced to Monday's championship the following year, Williams couldn't wait to get ahold of his friend.

"Sure enough, on Sunday, Roy tells me he'd like to give me his two tickets for the championship game," Ryan explained. "He said you can have anybody you want sit in one of the seats, but one has to be left open for Butch.

"So I gave one of the tickets to Ron Rainey, who coached me in high school and college, and the other sat empty. It was a really neat gesture. I was touched."

Outside the building, lower level tickets were creeping toward $1,000, but inside the grandiose brick barn, one of the best seats in the house was vacant: Section 140, Row A, Seat 13.

Butch Ryan, a 38-year regular at the Final Four who had passed away prior to the 2013-14 season, was there in spirit.

He would be one of many pulling for the Badgers that night.

Bo Ryan shows off the two championship game tickets that North Carolina's Roy Williams left him. One went to Ryan's former coach, the other seat sat empty in memory of his late father, Butch Ryan. *By Patrick Herb*

Wisconsin's historic win over Kentucky sent the two fan bases in opposite directions. The overwhelming Big Blue Nation that had dominated the semifinals was now flooding the market with tickets. Big Red was gobbling them up just as fast.

Badgers faithful who had missed Saturday's theatrics, like Class of 2001 alum Nathan Ballard, were not going to make the same mistake twice.

"We watched the Kentucky game at one of our houses in Chicago and when it ended we all just kind of looked at each other and said, 'We have to go Monday. No matter what it takes,'" Ballard said. "Wisconsin hasn't played in a national championship since 1941 and we all said, 'This could be it for our generation, you never know.'"

The 250-mile stretch of interstate from the Wisconsin border to Indianapolis began to resemble Regent Street in Madison with "America's Dairyland" license plates as far as you could see.

"On the drive to Indianapolis we'd see a car with Wisconsin license plates or a 'W' sticker in the window and we'd drive by and yell out to them or flash the 'W' out the window," Ballard continued. "We did that for maybe the first 15 minutes or so until we realized that basically every third car was Badgers fans. We'd stop at a gas station in a small Indiana town and it would be full of cars with Wisconsin fans heading to Indy."

By Monday afternoon, the Badgers had painted the town red. Indianapolis felt like Madison on a football Saturday. Bars were running out of Miller Lite, red and white tailgates popped up on every corner and it was difficult to discern who Wisconsin was even playing in the national championship.

"Everywhere you looked it was Badgers fans having a good time," Ballard added. "It seemed like one big Wisconsin family reunion. It really felt like being in Madison."

"People can talk all they want about Kentucky fans showing up at Final Fours, but nobody turned out like Wisconsin that weekend," ESPN broadcaster and Indianapolis resident Dan Dakich said. "I walked through downtown with a bunch of friends on Monday and Indy was ALL red. And every single person I saw looked like they were having fun."

Outside, the swarm of red was buzzing in the afterglow of beating Kentucky, but inside the quiet quarters of the Omni Hotel, the Badgers were busy preparing.

By the time Championship Monday rolled around, Indianapolis felt like Madison on a football Saturday. Tens of thousands of Badgers fans painted the town red.
By David Stluka

In the 48 hours between the semifinals and final, Ryan was

reminded countless times of the 1980 USA hockey team. That team is remembered for pulling off the "Miracle on Ice" by knocking off the heavily-favored Russians in the Olympics. Many forget that was only a semifinal win. Team USA still had to beat Finland in the gold medal game.

For the Badgers, beating Kentucky certainly wasn't a miracle, but the analogy rang true. UW had not yet reached the summit.

Truth be told, Ryan and company needed no such warning.

"After the Kentucky game I remember almost getting annoyed in the locker room by all the media congratulating us like we had won the whole thing," Gasser said. "We were fired up about beating Kentucky, don't get me wrong, but we knew we had another huge game left."

"We didn't go into the Kentucky game worrying about their streak or being undefeated," Dekker added. "Kentucky just happened to be the next team in front of us and another step to our ultimate goal. Duke in the championship was our goal. They had already beaten us once; we knew they were good."

Few games in the history of Wisconsin basketball have been hyped as much as Wisconsin's December 3 meeting with Duke in the 2014 Big Ten/ACC Challenge. The Badgers entered the game 7-0 and ranked No. 2 in the AP poll while the Blue Devils came to Madison with an identical 7-0 record and No. 2 ranking in the coaches poll.

The heavyweight fight also provided an individual matchup that was worth the price of admission, a battle that stacked up the two front runners for National Player of the Year against each other in Frank Kaminsky and Jahlil Okafor.

Duke would grab control in the second half thanks to a historic shooting performance. The Blue Devils connected on

Cell phone cameras capture every step as Frank Kaminsky emerges from the tunnel and takes the court at Lucas Oil Stadium for the national championship. *By Darron Cummings*

65 percent from the field, a Kohl Center record for a UW opponent. A three-point game with five minutes remaining, the Blue Devils used a 6-0 run to pull away with the 80-70 win.

Kaminsky would outscore Okafor 17 to 13, but little else went right for the Badgers. The home locker room was filled with disappointment, but the tenor was less about losing the game and more about not playing to potential.

"I was actually really optimistic after the

game," Nigel Hayes remembered. "If you looked at it, we came away knowing we could beat them. Sam and I virtually didn't play in the game (the duo combined for nine points), then throw in the fact that they shot an outrageous percentage and we were still right there with a couple minutes to go. We knew we played poorly."

"For how good Duke played and the way we stayed in the game despite not playing our best, it almost gave us confidence," Kaminsky said. "We knew if we played like

we're capable then we could beat the best, and we were looking forward to that chance."

"I still remember it," Hayes recalled months later. "Coach asked us before the game, 'Do you want to tell your kids and your grandkids someday that you played in the national championship or that you won the national championship?'"

That question would ring in the Badgers' ears right up until the time they took the floor at Lucas Oil Stadium. At that point, the soundtrack that took over was a roar from the red-stained crowd of 71,000 strong.

"It was like Kohl Center South in there," Dakich noted. "Wisconsin had the best support I've ever seen for a Final Four weekend."

"I've been to the last 15 Final Fours and I've been to every championship game," Big Ten Network analyst and former Illinois standout Stephen Bardo said. "I have never – I'll repeat, never – been in an atmosphere in a championship game like that. The Wisconsin fans traveled better than anybody I've ever seen."

The first national championship between No. 1 seeds since 2008 and a pick 'em betting line in Las Vegas, Wisconsin vs. Duke was boiling over with anticipation. By the first media timeout, the lead had already changed four times.

Neither team led by more than six points in the first half and a 31-31 tie at intermission seemed to indicate another instant classic was unfolding.

At the half, Ryan would remind the team of his pregame message, saying, "It's all right here for the taking. This is your chance. Be who we are and never change."

True to form, the Badgers were the aggressor to start the second half. Bronson Koenig drilled a 3 on the first possession before UW attacked the rim, scoring 10 of its next 12 points from inside the paint or at the free throw line. By the time Kaminsky laid in an inbounds pass from Gasser, the Badgers had built an impressive nine-point lead at 48-39 and forced Duke's Mike Krzyzewski to call a timeout.

Lucas Oil Stadium was officially rocking. As Kaminsky marched to the bench, he waved the frenzied crowd to its feet, thundering "Let's go!" to anyone that would listen. It had been

After a tie game at the half, Duje Dukan and the Badgers roared out to a nine-point lead with 13:17 left to play. *By Darron Cummings*

By Michael Conroy

74 years since Wisconsin had won a national championship in basketball and with 13:17 left to play, the Badgers seemed to be riding a wave of momentum into the history books.

"We were feeling confident, but there was a lot of time left," Gasser warned. "We just kept saying, 'We need to get stops.'"

"We were changing sides of the floor with the ball, touching the post, going inside and outside," Ryan said of his UW team that had scored 17 points in the first 10 possessions of the second half. "We also had freedom of movement in those first 30 minutes. Things would get a lot more physical later in the game and you have to match that. We probably didn't do as good of a job as we should have."

Wisconsin, which had committed just two fouls in the opening 20 minutes, had quickly racked up four in the first four minutes of the second half. An ominous sign for things to come.

Trailing by nine with two of its top three scorers (Okafor and Justise Winslow) on the bench with three fouls, Duke found an unlikely spark in freshman Grayson Allen. The McDonald's All-American who averaged just 4.4 points per game scored his team's next eight points and willed the Blue Devils back in the game.

Duke's surge continued as a three-point play by freshman Tyus Jones cut the deficit to one. Ryan gathered the refs and pleaded for a review of the foul call on Koenig, already the team's eighth infraction of the half. Ryan knew they wouldn't take a second look, but he was making a larger point of what he thought was the Blue Devils

initiating the contact on their drives.

An offensive foul on Duje Dukan moments later had the Badgers confounded. The carefree team that had been unflappable for 39 games suddenly seemed rattled.

"That was the only time all season I ever saw our guys get discouraged," Ryan would say later. "The way Duke was driving into them, they were coming back to the bench saying, 'Coach, what are we going to do?' And they had never asked me something like that in a huddle."

Wisconsin was taking on water but never stopped paddling. Back-to-back layups from Kaminsky and Sam Dekker put the Badgers ahead 58-56 with 4:28 remaining.

All season long UW had built an impeccable, Mariano Rivera-like reputation for closing out games. In fact, the team was a perfect 34-0 when leading or tied with five minutes remaining. Just two days earlier, the Badgers had reminded a nation how good they were at finishing when they erased a four-point deficit in the final four minutes with a 15-4 run vs. Kentucky.

On this night, Duke was just a little better. The freshman duo of Okafor and Jones would account for a 10-0 run to pull the Blue Devils ahead 66-58 with 1:24 left on the season. A Kaminsky 3 and a dunk from Hayes closed the gap to 3, but a crucial out-

▶Top: "That was the only time all season I ever saw our guys get discouraged. They were coming back to the bench saying, 'Coach, what are we going to do?'" – Bo Ryan *By David J. Phillip*

▶Bottom: Freshman Grayson Allen was the sparkplug for Duke, scoring eight consecutive points and helping the Blue Devils pull even at 54-54 with 7:05 remaining. *By David J. Phillip*

Frank Kaminsky capped off his sensational career with 21 points and 12 rebounds in his final game as a collegiate player. *By Chris Steppig*

of-bounds replay review that went against Wisconsin and a pair of Jones free throws would seal their fate.

As streamers popped and the Duke players celebrated in the background, Kaminsky and Gasser collapsed into each other's arms in front of the UW bench, holding back tears and holding onto the waning moments of their careers.

In his final game at Wisconsin, Kaminsky was outstanding. The consensus National Player of the Year had dominated Okafor, scoring around and through the future lottery pick. Kaminsky's collegiate curtain call of 21 points and 12 rebounds left no doubt that he had put together the most decorated season in UW annals.

"These guys are my family and I mean that literally," Kaminsky said with heartache at the postgame press conference. "I don't mean that hypothetically. I've never been closer to a group of guys in my entire life. From the coaching staff on down to every single player on this team. It's going to be hard to say goodbye."

"It's hard to explain the feelings postgame," Gasser said later. "We truly expected to win the game so when you realize that it didn't happen, it's kind of shocking and hard to swallow. The toughest

Wisconsin's magical ride came to end with a 68-63 loss. *By Michael Conroy*

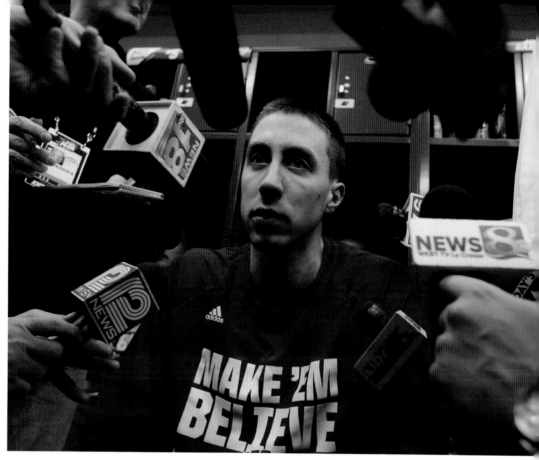

"It was like somebody threw a flashbang grenade into our locker room. You can see everything going on in slow motion but you don't hear anything but that piercing sound."
– Nigel Hayes   *By Michael Conroy*

part is realizing it's your last game as a Badger and last game playing with the group of guys that you've become so close to. It's not necessarily about the game, it's about the relationships coming to an end."

"I just couldn't believe it was over," Dekker added. "I was disappointed in myself and disappointed in letting people down, my teammates, my coaches. Across the board I think everybody felt they could have done something more to win that game."

The postgame locker room was a quiet mix of agony and anger, regret and heartache.

"I don't even really remember what was said," Hayes said. "At that point it was more like what you see in military movies when there is a flashbang and everything goes silent other than that high-pitched sound. You can see everything going on in slow motion but you don't hear anything but that piercing sound. I was sitting there and I knew people were talking, but I was just dazed thinking, 'We just lost the national championship game.' It was like somebody threw a flashbang grenade into our locker room."

The group that had brought so much joy to the month of March was now reduced to numbness. Ryan would step to the front of the lockerroom and peer at his emotionally defeated team.

"In our lives we're going to face adversity and tougher things than this," Ryan began quietly. "I know you're hurt and I know you're extremely disappointed, but hold your heads up high. You have a lot to be proud of – a lot that can never be taken from you.

"It will hit you someday what you guys have accomplished. You've had a great year and I've never been prouder of a team than this one."

Ryan paused knowing there wasn't much else to say in this moment.

"I want to say thank you," he finished. "Thanks for taking us all on this ride." ∎

AMERICA'S TEAM

"We will remember this team."

Two nights before Wisconsin started its historic march to the national championship game, the Badgers gathered at an indoor go-kart track just outside downtown Omaha. After zipping around the gnarly-shaped course, the team scurried over to a results board to check their times and relive the race.

Debates raged about whether or not Zak Showalter was the best driver or if he merely had the pole position. Players howled at the thought of Riley Dearring smashing into the wall and needing to be rescued. They playfully laughed at Duje Dukan's "responsible grandma driving."

Moved by the moment, Nigel Hayes got everyone's attention and pondered, "Guys... in a few years, we're going to remember moments like this and think, 'Man, we had a great time.' We're gonna miss this the most. There's going to be a time someday that you're going to look back on this and wish you could go back to that time."

Hayes' words hung for a second.

Then true to their nature and inability to take anything seriously besides basketball, his teammates fired back, "What!? Oh, shut up."

"That's such a soft and corny thing to say."

"That's like something out of *The Notebook* or something."

Laughter again filled the gasoline-saturated air and the Badgers sprinted back to the go-karts for race number two.

But Hayes was right. We will remember this team.

We will remember the school-record 36 wins. We will remember the Big Ten championships and back-to-back Final Fours. We will remember the most efficient offense on record. We will remember the collection of personalities

"They were an amazing show. The Badgers might want to forget their last game, but the nation won't soon forget them." Phil Taylor, *Sports Illustrated*   Courtesy of UW Athletics

"I can't ever recall seeing anything but pure joy out of them." Dan Dakich, ESPN
Courtesy of UW Athletics

that won the hearts of America. We will remember how refreshing and entertaining they were. We will remember them as a symbol of how great college teams used to be assembled, with a mix of youth and experience, stars and gritty role players, unheralded kids who blossomed at their own pace but collectively sang in unison.

"The word unique is overused, it literally means one of a kind," *Sporting News* columnist Mike DeCourcy explained. "I've covered 26 Final Fours, and as a group, this team was truly unique. The way they interacted with each other and media was unique, and one of a kind. This team was totally different in the way they handled pressure, the way they handled their shot. They handled it beautifully."

"I love the way they play basketball," ESPN analyst Dan Dakich added. "A lot of teams play well, but what I liked about Wisconsin was the way they interacted with each other. It was real. There was never a time when I saw anything negative towards a teammate. In fact, I can't ever recall seeing anything but pure joy out of them."

"I think people even beyond Badgers fans loved us because we were a team they could relate to," Frank Kaminsky theorized. "We were a bunch of guys that wanted to have fun and be kids. We weren't afraid to come out of our shells and show who we were. Deep down, don't we all want that?"

The impact this team had on the college basketball landscape was visible in the coverage of the team's final game. Never before had we seen so many stories written about the national runner-up.

Sports Illustrated's Brian Hamilton wrote, "Fans at Lucas Oil Stadium saw a victory for joy in basketball, for playing and living free and easy, without cynicism or bombast or an ego overload. Wisconsin confirmed you can be serious about a championship and hardly anything else. The Badgers are fun, a hardwood glee club, unburdened by a demand to be something other than who they are. If the weight of expectations fell upon Wisconsin, it would probably land on a whoopee cushion."

Sam Vecenis of CBS Sports wrote, "When history looks back on this team, it shouldn't simply be as 'the team that beat Kentucky in the Final Four.' It would be a disservice to this whimsical offensive juggernaut to diminish them to a footnote in history."

"They were an amazing show," Phil Taylor of *SI* added.

"The Badgers might want to forget their last game, but the nation won't soon forget them."

The Badgers dominated the streets of Indianapolis and the digital space as well. According to uberVU, a marketing platform that measures online impact, 68 percent of the internet conversation (social media, blogs, news stories, etc.) surrounding the Final Four centered on Wisconsin. Kentucky was a distant second at 14 percent.

As Fox Sports' Tim Brando tweeted, "Wisconsin's a great program and Bo Ryan's run the last two seasons resonates throughout sport."

"I've started to get perspective on what Badgers basketball means to the state and Wisconsin fans at large," Sam Dekker noted. "I know I don't grasp the whole magnitude of it yet, but when you hear about dogs and kids being named after you or you see our jerseys everywhere, it feels really cool to represent a state like that. I saw so many pictures of classrooms and schools wearing Wisconsin shirts and heard from schools making signs. People told me about the McDonald's and Culver's and places in Sheboygan changing their marquees to read 'Go Sam Go.' That stuff really makes you appreciate the support and makes you proud to represent them in a positive manner."

"Just walking down the street, wherever you are in the state, and hearing people tell us 'thank you' for what we did for them is really special," Josh Gasser added. "It's more than I ever dreamed and I'm grateful for the opportunity to represent Wisconsin."

"After the season the chancellor had the team over to her house and they were thanking us for bringing a community together," Hayes said. "I was like, 'Really, we brought the community together?' It kind of sunk in a bit that we were doing some pretty big things."

"You see people that are thanking you, and at the same time, you're thanking them for the support," Dekker went on. "I was talking to someone the other day, saying there's nothing more you could ever want out of a college experience than UW-Madison. Whether its academics, fan support, sports, scenery, it's everything you want. The things we've been able to do here for this university with 'Wisconsin' on our chest is something we take pride in, and being able to have success is really cool. I feel very fortunate to have been able to go to UW and be in Madison."

They weren't the only ones feeling fortunate.

"I'll share with you a story," longtime ESPN announcer Mike Tirico said. "On Friday of the Big Ten tournament my partner Dan Dakich and I were getting set to call our final Badgers game of the season. Long before the game, the Wisconsin players were just hanging out on the court, even before the baskets were available to them. I don't ever root for teams or care who wins, but I remember feeling compelled to go up to the group and say, 'Good luck today. It's been a pleasure covering you. Thank you for letting me be able to cover you guys.' In my role, I always felt a warmth with that group that was more than any other."

Letters and phone calls of the same sentiment poured into the men's basketball office at the Kohl Center. Each message filled with pride and gratitude.

"The amount of people we have heard from is overwhelming," Bo Ryan said. "People fell in love with these guys and their personalities and the team. America loved this team for how they went about their business from the time they arrived on campus to the time they're going to leave. They respected what these players represented."

In the weeks after the season, Kaminsky's whirlwind tour took him to Los Angeles, New York, Chicago, Washington D.C. and seemingly all points in between. Everywhere he went, he encountered people who were moved by the Badgers.

"I can't count all the people who have come up to me to say congrats, or thanks, or just wanting to say hi," Kaminsky said. "It happens everywhere I go. Even at the White House Correspondents' Dinner when I sat with Bill Belichick, he wanted to talk about our team. You realize the impact when you find Badgers fans clear across the country."

Maybe that's what Make 'Em Believe was about. For a magical four weeks in March and April, the Badgers, in a way, unified a nation. They showed us that being magnificent in our craft doesn't have to come at the expense of respect and laughter. In fact, in some instances, those are the formula for success.

That's something we can all believe. ∎

"It's been a pleasure covering you. Thank you for letting me be able to cover you guys." Mike Tirico, ESPN *Courtesy of UW Athletics*

EPILOGUE *by Bo Ryan*

When I first got to Madison as an assistant coach under Bill Cofield it was 1976. It was nearly 40 years ago, but when you look at the state of Wisconsin Basketball, it feels like nearly 140 years have passed. My first season on the job we went 11-16. Four years later, in 1980, when we finished with a winning record we felt like we had conquered a mountain.

Back then, we sat around and dreamed of making the NIT, let alone the NCAA tournament. So as I sit here now and reflect on the health of our program, I can't help but feel proud, grateful and blessed all at the same time.

But the thing that brings me the most pride is hearing from countless Badgers fans and feeling the impact our guys have had on folks. The amount of letters and messages that have come through our office has been simply amazing. We've heard from 90-year-olds that have followed the team religiously their entire life to the 25-year-old who recently graduated from UW and loves to brag about his alma mater.

We heard from a fan who lives in Canada. He has never attended a Badgers game or even been to the state of Wisconsin, but loves our program to the point that he shed a tear when our season ended. Or there was the story I heard from a friend who drove to Indianapolis for the Final Four with his daughter. He told me that after we beat Kentucky his daughter gave him a hug and said, "This is the greatest moment ever." He said it was unbelievable and they had a bonding moment over it.

I've heard from a lot of people who have said that Kentucky win will be one of those events where they will always be able to remember where they were and who they were with.

By Michael Conroy

By David Stluka

in the way he did; Traevon Jackson's leadership even when he was down; Duje Dukan, who had graduated and could have transferred and probably started for several other colleges, but he wanted to stay at Wisconsin and be a part of another run. Each and every one of the players on the team had an impact on our success.

We were always pulling the same direction. That's the strength of the University of Wisconsin and why I've stayed in this state as long as I have. It's one of the reasons I have always wanted to be here and work at an institution that believes in the right values and believes in what is best for the student-athlete.

At Wisconsin, it's a collective effort. The athletic department, the administrators, the board of regents and certainly the passionate and supportive fans, everybody is a part of this. I'm honored to represent that. I hope you are, too. ∎

Those moments in life are priceless and I'm honored to have a small part in them.

As much as any team I've ever been fortunate enough to coach, this group epitomized the "work hard, play hard" ideal. I thanked them in the locker room after the national championship. I thanked them for letting me roam the sidelines and for a heck of a season.

Every team I coach has an impact on me and changes me in some way, especially this one. I really had fun this year.

This team was full of characters that will have a lasting impression on me and hopefully Badgers fans everywhere: Frank Kaminsky returning to be part of something special and the way he handled his development and success; Sam Dekker maturing every day; the example Josh Gasser showed daily; Nigel Hayes going from a non 3-point shooter to a guy that had to be guarded everywhere; Bronson Koenig filling

By David Stluka

2014-15 Wisconsin Men's Basketball

Wisconsin Combined Team Statistics (as of April 06, 2015)

All Games

Overall Record: 36-4 Conference: 16-2 Home: 15-1 Away: 10-2 Neutral: 1-1

##	Player	gp-gs	min	avg	Total fg-fga	fg%	3-Point 3fg-fga	3fg%	F-Throw ft-fta	ft%	Rebounds off	def	tot	avg	pf	dq	a	to	blk	stl	pts	avg
44	Kaminsky, Frank	39-39	1311	33.6	267-488	.547	42-101	.416	156-200	.780	58	262	320	8.2	65	0	103	63	57	33	732	18.8
15	Dekker, Sam	40-40	1239	31.0	213-406	.525	50-151	.331	80-113	.708	77	143	220	5.5	42	0	49	36	18	21	556	13.9
10	Hayes, Nigel	40-40	1318	33.0	166-334	.497	40-101	.396	125-168	.744	85	162	247	6.2	76	1	79	51	16	34	497	12.4
24	Koenig, Bronson	40-24	1152	28.8	115-278	.414	62-153	.405	56-69	.812	19	51	70	1.8	64	2	98	33	8	9	348	8.7
12	Jackson, Traevon	21-17	506	24.1	60-139	.432	11-39	.282	40-47	.851	4	31	35	1.7	27	0	54	32	3	19	171	8.1
21	Gasser, Josh	40-40	1320	33.0	77-174	.443	49-126	.389	62-75	.827	29	110	139	3.5	90	1	70	21	8	30	265	6.6
13	Dukan, Duje	38-0	605	15.9	60-155	.387	29-91	.319	31-46	.674	28	70	98	2.6	48	0	24	25	3	8	180	4.7
03	Showalter, Zak	35-0	266	7.6	23-53	.434	2-14	.143	24-27	.889	18	27	45	1.3	38	0	16	5	4	10	72	2.1
30	Brown, Vitto	34-0	214	6.3	26-59	.441	0-0	.000	10-17	.588	12	31	43	1.3	38	0	7	15	8	8	62	1.8
35	Dearring, Riley	15-0	39	2.6	4-10	.400	3-7	.429	0-1	.000	0	4	4	0.3	5	0	1	6	0	1	11	0.7
05	Moesch, Aaron	14-0	28	2.0	2-7	.286	0-1	.000	0-2	.000	2	4	6	0.4	4	0	3	2	1	0	4	0.3
04	Ferris, Matt	9-0	17	1.9	1-3	.333	0-1	.000	0-0	.000	3	2	5	0.6	1	0	0	1	1	1	2	0.2
02	Smith, Jordan	14-0	35	2.5	0-9	.000	0-5	.000	0-0	.000	1	1	2	0.1	3	0	0	0	0	0	0	0.0
	Team										47	57	104					6				
	Total.........	40	8050		1014-2115	.479	288-790	.365	584-765	.763	383	955	1338	33.5	501	4	504	296	127	174	2900	72.5
	Opponents.....	40	8050		896-2092	.428	202-538	.375	333-469	.710	297	809	1106	27.7	723	-	359	378	84	163	2327	58.2

SCHEDULE & RESULTS

	Date	Opponent		Score	Att.
	11/14/14	NORTHERN KENTUCKY	W	62-31	17279
	11/16/14	CHATTANOOGA	W	89-45	17279
	11/19/14	GREEN BAY	W	84-60	17279
	11/22/14	BOISE STATE	W	78-54	17279
	11/26/14	vs UAB	W	72-43	2633
	11/27/14	vs Georgetown	W	68-65	3204
	11/28/14	vs Oklahoma	W	69-56	2667
	12/03/14	DUKE	L	70-80	17279
	12/06/14	at Marquette	W	49-38	18573
	12/10/14	at Milwaukee	W	93-54	10120
	12/13/14	NICHOLLS STATE	W	86-43	17279
	12/22/14	at California	W	68-56	11877
	12/28/14	BUFFALO	W	68-56	17279
*	12/31/14	PENN STATE	W	89-72	17279
*	01/04/15	at Northwestern	W	81-58	8117
*	01/07/15	PURDUE	W	62-55	17279
*	01/11/15	at Rutgers	L	62-67	6987
*	01/15/15	NEBRASKA	W	70-55	17279
*	01/20/15	IOWA	W	82-50	17279
*	01/24/15	at Michigan	Wot	69-64	12579
*	01/31/15	at Iowa	W	74-63	15400

	Date	Opponent		Score	Att.
*	02/03/15	INDIANA	W	92-78	17279
*	02/07/15	NORTHWESTERN	W	65-50	17279
*	02/10/15	at Nebraska	W	65-55	15701
*	02/15/15	ILLINOIS	W	68-49	17279
*	02/18/15	at Penn State	W	55-47	7132
*	02/21/15	MINNESOTA	W	63-53	17279
*	02/24/15	at Maryland	L	53-59	17950
*	03/01/15	MICHIGAN STATE	W	68-61	17279
*	03/05/15	at Minnesota	W	76-63	14625
*	03/8/15	at Ohio State	W	72-48	18077
	03/13/15	vs Michigan	W	71-60	17290
	03/14/15	vs Purdue	W	71-51	18088
	03/15/15	vs Michigan State	Wot	80-69	17213
	03/20/15	vs Coastal Carolina	W	86-72	17534
	03/22/15	vs Oregon	W	72-65	17563
	03/26/15	vs North Carolina	W	79-72	18809
	03/28/15	vs Arizona	W	85-78	19125
	04/04/15	vs Kentucky	W	71-64	72238
	04/06/15	vs Duke	L	63-68	71149

* = Conference game

PATRICK HERB

Patrick Herb, an alumnus of UW-Madison and seven-year veteran of the Kansas City Chiefs public relations staff, is the assistant director of athletic communications for the Badgers. He serves as the lead public relations contact for Wisconsin Basketball and is the sideline reporter for the Wisconsin Radio Network's broadcasts of Badger football. Herb and his wife, Lindsay, are both Appleton, Wis., natives and currently reside in Verona with their sons, Tyler and Austin.